JOSEPH

A Type of the 6th Seal and the Feasts

Eric C. Alger

Eternal Roots LTD

Copyright © 2024 Eternal Roots LTD

All rights reserved. No part of this publication may be reproduced, distributed, or transmitted in any form or by any means, including photocopying, recording, or other electronic or mechanical methods, without the prior written permission of the publisher, except in the case of brief quotations embodied in critical reviews and certain other non-commercial uses permitted by copyright law.

For permission requests, please contact the publisher at the address below:

ETERNAL ROOTS LTD
5900 BALCONES DR STE 100
AUSTIN, TX 78731
www.eternalrootsltd.com

First Edition: November 2024

CONTENTS

Title Page
Copyright
Unlocking the Prophetic Layers of Joseph's Life — 5
Preparing for the Journey: Joseph's Story in Three Parts — 7
Part 1: Joseph's Life and Trials—A Prophetic Foreshadowing of the 6th Seal — 10
Chapter 1: Favored Son, Betrayed Brother — 13
Chapter 2: The Pit and the 6th Seal—Shaken but Not Destroyed — 20
Chapter 3: From Prison to Power—The Endurance of the Saints — 24
Chapter 4: Managing the Famine—The Wisdom of Joseph — 29
Chapter 5: The Feast of Atonement—Forgiveness and Reconciliation — 34
Chapter 6: Restoration of the Family—The Spiritual Temple — 40
Chapter 7: Joseph—A Life of Endurance, Preparation, and Reconciliation — 46
Chapter 8: Reflecting on Joseph's Life and Trials—A Foreshadowing of the 6th Seal — 53
Part 2: Joseph and the Feasts—Prophetic Insights from the Feast of Trumpets and Atonement — 61
Chapter 9: Joseph's Journey from Suffering to Sovereignty — 62

Chapter 10: The Feast of Trumpets—A Call to Spiritual Preparation … 73

Chapter 11: Provision in the Famine—Joseph as a Prophetic Provider … 84

Chapter 12: The Unveiling of God's Plan … 95

Chapter 13: Restoration of the Family—The Spiritual Temple … 114

Chapter 14: Joseph … 123

Chapter 15: Reflecting on Joseph's Life and Trials—A Foreshadowing of the 6th Seal … 134

Part 3: The Deliverer and the Preserver—Joseph as a Type of Christ … 144

Chapter 16: Joseph as a Foreshadowing of the Messiah's Role in Deliverance and Preservation … 145

Chapter 17: Joseph and the Sovereignty of God … 152

Chapter 18: Joseph and the Reversal of Fortune … 159

Chapter 19: Joseph as a Type of the Suffering Servant (Isaiah 53) … 166

Chapter 20: Joseph's Forgiveness and Restoration as a Type of the New Covenant … 174

Chapter 21: Joseph's Role in Preserving the Lineage of Israel … 182

Chapter 22: Joseph as a Type of Intercessor … 190

Chapter 23: The Typology of Dreams: Revelation and God's Plan … 198

Chapter 24: Joseph as a Type of the Righteous Sufferer (Psalm 22) … 207

Chapter 25: Joseph—A Type of Redemption and Christ … 215

Epilogue … 224

Step into Your Role as an Intercessor … 226

Receiving Jesus: A Path to Eternal Life	228
Glossary of Terms	233
Suggested Reading	237
Guided Reflections	239
Scripture Index	263

Dedication

To all those who walk through trials with faith, trusting that every season of hardship is a preparation for something greater.

To my son, Benjamin, may you always see God's hand at work, even in the most difficult moments, and know that He has a plan for your life beyond what you can imagine.

And to Chad, my brother—this is for the warriors who rise again, for the broken who find healing, and for the lost who find their way home.

May the story of Joseph remind us all that though we may be shaken, we are never abandoned, and that God's promises endure beyond the darkest of days.

To my nephew Lucas Allen, may the Lord be your guide and keeper, filling your heart with wisdom and courage as you journey through life. Like Joseph, who rose with faith and resilience, may you too grow in strength, steadfast in hope and purpose. May God's light shine through you, bringing joy and inspiration to all you encounter. May His love be your foundation, His peace your guard, and His promises your strength. In all things, may you know His unfailing grace and walk in His favor, now and always. Amen.

- Eric Alger

Acknowledgments

First and foremost, I thank my Heavenly Father, whose hand of providence guides every step of this journey. Just as Joseph's life was shaped by trials and triumphs for a greater purpose, so too has this book been shaped by His sovereign will. I am constantly reminded that I did not choose Him, but He chose me, drawing me by His Spirit and placing within me the desire to seek His truth. It is humbling to recognize that before I ever set my hand to this work, He had already ordained it.

I extend my deepest gratitude to those who have supported and encouraged me throughout this process. Your wisdom, prayers, and insights have been invaluable, and I am grateful for the role each of you has played in the fulfillment of this work.

Lastly, to those who may never know their impact on this journey—whether through a kind word, thoughtful action, or silent support—this book would not have been possible without you. You were part of God's providence, and for that, I am truly thankful.

To God be the glory, who sustains all things and works all things together for good, according to His purpose.

Preface

The story of Joseph is one that has captivated believers and scholars for generations. It is a narrative woven with the threads of betrayal, resilience, forgiveness, and divine purpose. Yet, beyond its immediate appeal as a dramatic tale of a young man rising from the depths of suffering to the heights of power, Joseph's life reveals a profound layer of prophetic symbolism. His story is not only a historical account but also a foreshadowing—a type—of the ultimate redemption found in Christ.

As I began studying Joseph's journey, I became increasingly aware of how deeply it reflects God's overarching plan for humanity. Joseph's experiences mirror the trials of faith, the promise of deliverance, and the call to live in harmony with God's will. With each event in his life, Joseph's story illuminates themes that extend into the heart of the New Testament, drawing lines that connect the Old Testament shadows to the realities unveiled in Christ.

This book is my attempt to unpack these layers, to explore how Joseph's life serves as a precursor to the mission of Jesus, particularly through the lens of the prophetic and redemptive feasts ordained by God. These feasts—the Feast of Trumpets, the Feast of Atonement, and others—point forward to Christ's work and reveal God's design for reconciliation, forgiveness, and ultimate unity with His people. By linking Joseph's life to these feasts and prophetic symbols, we see a blueprint of God's love, His call to repentance, and His promise of restoration.

In a world that often feels broken and divided, I believe Joseph's story provides more than just historical insight; it offers a path for modern believers to walk in faith, to endure trials, and to find strength in God's promises. My hope is that this book will inspire you to see beyond the surface of Joseph's story, to understand the depth of God's redemptive work, and to apply these eternal truths in your own life.

Thank you for joining me on this journey. May Joseph's story and the symbolism within it draw you closer to God and encourage you to live in the light of His redemption.

UNLOCKING THE PROPHETIC LAYERS OF JOSEPH'S LIFE

The story of Joseph, a figure of both profound suffering and extraordinary redemption, is one of the most captivating narratives in the Bible. But beyond the well-known tale of a favored son betrayed by his brothers and later elevated to power, lies a deeper prophetic message—a message that stretches into the very fabric of end-time prophecy.

This book unveils the striking parallels between Joseph's trials and the events prophesied in the 6th Seal of the Book of Revelation, offering fresh insights that many traditional theological works overlook. It goes beyond viewing Joseph's life as mere history; instead, it positions his journey as a powerful typological foreshadowing of Christ and the cosmic events that will shape the world in the last days.

By drawing connections between Joseph's betrayal, imprisonment, and eventual rise to authority with the judgment, mercy, and restoration of the end times, this manuscript brings new clarity to the eschatological significance of his life. Through the lens of Jewish feasts and prophecy, Joseph's story becomes a blueprint for understanding the unfolding of God's redemptive plan for humanity.

What makes this book unique is its ability to blend Joseph's personal narrative with intricate prophetic themes, revealing how his life serves as a shadow of future events—offering readers both a profound theological exploration and a practical guide for enduring faith.

Prepare to journey through the life of Joseph as never before, uncovering layers of meaning that resonate not only with the past but with the future of God's prophetic timeline.

PREPARING FOR THE JOURNEY: JOSEPH'S STORY IN THREE PARTS

This book is designed to explore the life of Joseph through two complementary lenses: his personal journey and its prophetic significance. By examining Joseph's story alongside key themes from biblical prophecy and the Jewish feasts, we uncover layers of meaning that extend beyond the historical narrative.

Part 1: Joseph's Life And Trials—A Prophetic Foreshadowing Of The 6Th Seal

In Part 1, we delve into Joseph's early life, marked by favoritism and jealousy within his family, which ultimately leads to betrayal by his brothers. His journey from betrayal to a place of power mirrors the tribulations represented by the 6th Seal in Revelation, characterized by upheaval and testing. Each chapter focuses on key stages in Joseph's life—his descent into the pit, his endurance in prison, and his rise to power—reflecting the endurance and faith required of believers as they face trials in the end times. This section lays the foundation for understanding Joseph not just as a historical figure but as a prophetic symbol of hope and resilience amidst cosmic trials.

and testing. Each chapter focuses on key stages in Joseph's life —his descent into the pit, his endurance in prison, and his rise to power, which reflect the endurance and faith required of believers as they face tribulations in the end times. This section sets the foundation for understanding Joseph not just as a historical figure, but as a prophetic type symbolizing hope and resilience amidst cosmic trials.

Part 2: Joseph And The Feasts—Prophetic Insights From The Feast Of Trumpets And Atonement

Part 2 deepens the exploration by connecting Joseph's story with the Jewish Feasts of Trumpets and Atonement. His role in managing Egypt's resources during the famine reflects the call for spiritual preparation associated with the Feast of Trumpets, a time of awakening and readiness for divine intervention. His reconciliation with his brothers embodies themes of repentance and forgiveness celebrated in the Feast of Atonement. Here, Joseph emerges as a savior figure, mirroring Christ's role in gathering and restoring God's people and pointing toward end-time events where God's plan for reconciliation and redemption reaches its fulfillment.

Part 3: The Deliverer And The Preserver—Joseph As A Type Of Christ

In Part 3, Joseph's life serves as a powerful foreshadowing of the Messiah's redemptive work. This section examines his role as a deliverer who preserves life in a time of crisis, drawing clear parallels to Christ's mission of spiritual salvation. Joseph's role as a reconciler prefigures the ultimate reconciliation brought by Christ, whose death and resurrection restore humanity's relationship with God. Through his story, Joseph offers readers a glimpse into the larger framework of redemption, highlighting the promise of restoration, deliverance, and eternal hope that

God extends through His Son.

PART 1: JOSEPH'S LIFE AND TRIALS —A PROPHETIC FORESHADOWING OF THE 6TH SEAL

Joseph—A Life Beyond Dreams

The story of Joseph, son of Jacob, is one of the most captivating narratives in the Bible. It is a tale filled with triumph and tragedy, betrayal and reconciliation, faith and divine providence. His journey—from the favored son, to a slave in Egypt, to the second most powerful man in the land—has inspired countless readers for generations. Yet, beyond the surface of his life's events lies a deeper prophetic significance. Joseph's life is not just a historical account; it is also a profound spiritual symbol and a prophetic foreshadowing of the events that will unfold in the end times.

The Bible often uses the lives of its key figures to convey hidden spiritual truths and mysteries. In Joseph, we find a perfect type and shadow of what is to come—the 6th Seal, the

Feast of Trumpets, and the Feast of Atonement. These prophetic themes, found throughout the pages of Scripture, are intimately connected to Joseph's story. His life becomes a mirror reflecting the divine plan for God's people, the trials and tribulations they will face, and the ultimate deliverance and reconciliation that God promises through Christ.

Joseph's story is a narrative of faith under fire. Betrayed by his own brothers, sold into slavery, falsely accused, and imprisoned—his life appears to be a series of devastating setbacks. But behind each hardship, God's hand was at work, orchestrating a much greater plan. What seemed like Joseph's darkest moments were, in reality, paving the way for his eventual rise to power, a position that allowed him to save his family and countless others from a devastating famine. This pattern of divine providence is not unique to Joseph; it is a reflection of the ultimate deliverance that will come through Christ.

In this book, we will explore the life of Joseph through both a historical and prophetic lens. We will see how Joseph's story not only serves as a remarkable example of faith, forgiveness, and perseverance but also how it foreshadows key biblical events. The **6th Seal** from the Book of Revelation, with its imagery of cosmic upheaval, finds its reflection in Joseph's early life, where everything he knew was shattered. The **Feast of Trumpets**, a call to spiritual awakening and preparation, can be seen in Joseph's interpretation of dreams and his foresight in preparing for famine. Finally, the **Feast of Atonement**, a day of reconciliation and forgiveness, is beautifully mirrored in Joseph's forgiveness of his brothers and the restoration of his family.

This book aims to uncover these layers of meaning and show that Joseph's life is more than just a story of personal triumph. It is a prophetic type of what is to come—pointing us toward the end times and the ultimate fulfillment of God's promises through Jesus Christ. By the end of this journey, you will not only gain a deeper understanding of Joseph's life but also a greater appreciation for how the Bible weaves together history, prophecy, and theology into a unified, divine narrative.

Let us now turn to the pages of Genesis and begin our exploration of **Joseph—A Life Beyond Dreams**.

CHAPTER 1: FAVORED SON, BETRAYED BROTHER

The story of Joseph begins in Genesis 37, where we are introduced to him as the favored son of his father, Jacob. This favoritism is not subtle—it is made clear by the special coat of many colors that Jacob gives to Joseph, a symbol of his unique place in the family. At just 17 years old, Joseph is already set apart, not only by his father's love but also by the dreams he has, which seem to suggest a future where he will rise above his brothers. To his siblings, however, these dreams are a sign of arrogance and ambition, fueling their jealousy and resentment.

The dynamics within Jacob's family are fraught with tension, and Joseph's favored status does nothing to ease the bitterness that has been growing among his brothers. In this family, we see the seeds of division that will soon lead to betrayal. But beneath the surface of this family drama, there is a divine plan unfolding—a plan that will take Joseph from the pit of betrayal to the pinnacle of power in Egypt.

Joseph's dreams are not just the musings of a young boy. They are prophetic visions, given by God, that foretell not only his personal rise to prominence but also the greater role he will play in the salvation of his family. In his dreams, he sees himself in a position of leadership, with his brothers and even his parents bowing down to him. Naturally, this stirs up anger and jealousy in his brothers. They already feel inferior due to the special attention Jacob gives to Joseph, and these dreams only add fuel to the fire. To them, Joseph's dreams are not a revelation from God but a display of his pride, his belief that he is better than them.

Yet, as often happens with God's plans, the road to that fulfillment is not smooth. Before Joseph can rise, he must first fall, and that fall begins with the betrayal of his own brothers. One day, when Joseph is sent by his father to check on his brothers who are tending sheep in the fields, the brothers seize the opportunity to rid themselves of the dreamer. Stripping him of his precious coat, they throw him into a pit with the intention of leaving him for dead. But instead, they sell him into slavery to a caravan of Ishmaelites heading to Egypt. The dreamer, once favored and protected, is now a slave in a foreign land.

The act of selling Joseph into slavery is not just an act of familial betrayal—it is a moment of cosmic significance. In this moment, we see the first echoes of the **6th Seal** in the Book of Revelation, a time of great shaking and tribulation. Just as Joseph's life is turned upside down by this violent act of betrayal, so too does the 6th Seal describe a time of cosmic upheaval. The earth quakes, the sun darkens, the moon turns to blood, and the stars fall from the sky (Revelation 6:12-14). This is a time of chaos and uncertainty, when everything familiar is shattered. In Joseph's life, his world is similarly shaken—he goes from being the favored son to a slave, seemingly abandoned by his family and by God.

In both the story of Joseph and the prophetic imagery of the 6th Seal, we see a pattern of apparent destruction giving way to divine purpose. The shaking of the heavens and the earth during the 6th Seal is not the final act but a prelude to something greater. In Joseph's life, his betrayal and descent into slavery are not the end of the story; they are the beginning of a much larger plan. God is not absent in Joseph's trials—He is working behind the scenes, shaping events in ways that will not only save Joseph but also preserve the future of the nation of Israel.

The Depth Of Betrayal

Joseph's betrayal is one of the most painful aspects of his story. He is not wronged by strangers, but by his own flesh and blood. His brothers, who should have protected him, instead conspired to destroy him. This betrayal echoes the broader theme of humanity's betrayal of God, a theme that runs throughout Scripture. Just as Joseph was sold by his brothers, humanity, in its sin, has turned away from God, betraying the One who created and loved them.

This act of betrayal also foreshadows Christ's betrayal at the hands of Judas. Like Joseph, Christ was sold for silver—30 pieces of silver—and was handed over to those who sought to destroy Him. In both Joseph and Christ, we see a pattern of betrayal followed by redemption. The betrayal, while painful, is part of the larger plan that God is orchestrating for the salvation of His people.

For Joseph, the betrayal is devastating. Not only is he stripped of his favored status, but he is also torn away from his family and everything he has ever known. He is cast into a foreign land, sold as a slave, and seemingly forgotten. Yet, even in this moment of utter despair, God's hand is at work. The caravan of Ishmaelites that takes Joseph to Egypt is not a random group of traders; they are part of the divine plan that will bring Joseph to the place where he is meant to be. Egypt, the land of his enslavement, will one day become the land of his triumph.

The Role Of The 6Th Seal: Shaking And Preparation

The connection between Joseph's betrayal and the **6th Seal** is significant. The 6th Seal represents a time of cosmic upheaval, a moment when the foundations of the world are shaken. The earth quakes, the sky is darkened, and the natural order is disrupted. In the same way, Joseph's life is shaken to its core. He goes from being the favored son to a slave in a foreign land, cut off from his family and everything he knows.

But the shaking of the 6th Seal, like the shaking of Joseph's life, is not without purpose. In both cases, the shaking is a form of preparation. In Revelation, the 6th Seal marks the beginning of the end, a time when the world is being prepared for the return of Christ and the establishment of God's kingdom. In Joseph's life, his betrayal and descent into slavery are the beginning of a journey that will prepare him for the role that God has for him. His time in Egypt, though painful and difficult, is part of the process of shaping him into the leader that he will become.

Joseph's trials are a form of refinement, a period of testing that prepares him for the future. In the same way, the shaking of the 6th Seal is a time of testing for the world, a moment when the faithful are called to endure and hold fast to their faith. Just as Joseph remained faithful to God in the midst of his trials, believers are called to remain faithful during the tribulation of the last days.

Endurance And Redemption

As Joseph's story unfolds, we will see how his endurance through suffering leads to his eventual redemption. Though he is betrayed and sold into slavery, Joseph does not give up. He remains faithful to God, even when it seems that God has forgotten him. This faithfulness is key to his eventual rise to power in Egypt, where he will become a ruler and a savior for his family and the nations around him.

The theme of endurance is also central to the events of the

6th Seal. The world will be shaken, and many will fall away in fear. But those who remain faithful will see the fulfillment of God's promises. Just as Joseph's endurance through betrayal and slavery led to his exaltation, so too will the endurance of the faithful during the tribulation lead to their ultimate redemption.

The Divine Plan Unfolds

As we leave Joseph in the hands of the Ishmaelites, sold as a slave and far from home, we are reminded that this is only the beginning of his journey. Though it seems as if Joseph's life is over, God's plan is just beginning to unfold. Joseph's betrayal will lead to his eventual rise to power, where he will save not only Egypt but also his own family.

In our own lives, we may face moments of betrayal, rejection, and suffering that feel like the end of the story. But just as in Joseph's life, these moments are often the beginning of a larger divine plan. God uses even the darkest moments to shape us for something greater. As we move forward in Joseph's story, we will see how his steadfast faith in the face of suffering paves the way for God's ultimate plan of redemption—not just for Joseph, but for the entire nation of Israel.

A Foreshadowing Of The 6Th Seal

Joseph's story, with its themes of betrayal, suffering, and redemption, serves as a powerful foreshadowing of the events described in the 6th Seal. Just as Joseph's life was shaken and turned upside down, so too will the world be shaken during the tribulation of the last days. But in both cases, the shaking is not the end—it is a form of preparation, a way of refining and purifying God's people for the greater work that is to come.

As we continue to explore Joseph's life, we will see how

his experiences in Egypt—his time in slavery, his unjust imprisonment, and his eventual rise to power—mirror the trials and tribulations that God's people will face before the final deliverance. But for now, we leave Joseph in the hands of the Ishmaelites, sold as a slave, far from home, and seemingly far from the fulfillment of his dreams. Yet, even in the distance, the divine plan is already unfolding.

Chapter 1: Study Questions For Reflection

Favored Son, Betrayed Brother:

1. In what ways does Joseph's early life reflect the spiritual trials we face when we are set apart by God?
2. How can jealousy and envy disrupt relationships within families and communities? What lessons can we learn from Joseph's brothers' actions?
3. Reflect on a time when you felt betrayed. How did you handle the situation, and where did you see God's hand at work, even when it was difficult?
4. What do Joseph's dreams reveal about God's sovereign plan, even in the midst of difficult circumstances?

CHAPTER 2: THE PIT AND THE 6TH SEAL—SHAKEN BUT NOT DESTROYED

Joseph's descent into the pit, followed by his sale into slavery, marks the beginning of a period in his life where everything he knows is torn away. He is thrust into a foreign land with no allies, no protection, and seemingly no future. It is here that Joseph's life aligns most closely with the imagery of the 6th Seal in Revelation, which speaks of great shaking and turmoil. This phase of Joseph's life is about endurance through tribulation—a tribulation that seems overwhelming but is, in fact, preparing him for a greater purpose.

In Revelation 6, the opening of the 6th Seal unleashes a series of cataclysmic events that shake both heaven and earth. The earth quakes, the sun turns black, the moon becomes as blood, and the stars fall from the sky. These signs speak of a time of judgment and upheaval, a moment when the stability of the world is turned upside down. For those experiencing it, this tribulation seems like the end—but as Revelation shows, it is only a precursor to deliverance.

Joseph's life in Egypt begins with a similar sense of devastation. He is sold to Potiphar, a high-ranking official in Pharaoh's service, and becomes a mere servant in Potiphar's household. The once-favored son of Jacob is now at the mercy of another man's orders. It would have been easy for Joseph to despair, to question where God was in all of this, or to lose hope entirely. Yet, remarkably, he does not. Joseph remains faithful and diligent, trusting that God is still with him despite his circumstances.

This period of Joseph's life offers a powerful example of how to endure tribulation without losing faith. In the same way that the **6th Seal** calls for believers to remain steadfast through the shaking of the heavens and the earth, Joseph's experience in Egypt calls for endurance through personal trials. Though everything around him has changed—his family is gone, his freedom is taken away—Joseph's faith remains unshaken. This enduring faith will be the key to his future success.

While serving in Potiphar's household, Joseph's character and abilities begin to shine. Potiphar notices that everything Joseph touches prospers, and he entrusts him with more and more responsibility until Joseph is made overseer of Potiphar's entire household. This rise within the household is a foreshadowing of what is to come in Joseph's life, but it is also a reminder that even in the midst of trials, God's favor is present. Though Joseph is still a slave, he is being prepared for something greater. His faithfulness in small things is laying the groundwork for his eventual leadership over much larger responsibilities.

But just as Joseph begins to rise, another trial looms. Potiphar's wife, attracted to Joseph, tries repeatedly to seduce him. When Joseph refuses her advances, remaining true to his moral convictions, she falsely accuses him of assault. This lie results in Joseph being thrown into prison, an even deeper descent into tribulation.

Once again, Joseph's world is shaken. He has done nothing

wrong, and yet he finds himself imprisoned. This false accusation and unjust punishment can be seen as another reflection of the **6th Seal**, where the faithful must endure hardship and persecution even though they are innocent. For Joseph, this is a moment of profound testing—a test of faith, of patience, and of character.

In prison, however, Joseph's faith remains firm. Just as he prospered in Potiphar's house, so too does he find favor in the eyes of the prison warden, who puts Joseph in charge of the other prisoners. Joseph's ability to rise even in the lowest of circumstances shows us that God's providence is always at work, even when life seems to be at its darkest. Like the events following the **6th Seal**, where the shaking of the earth is followed by the unveiling of God's greater plan, Joseph's tribulations are leading toward a larger redemption.

This period in prison also serves as a powerful parallel to the **6th Seal's** imagery of the sun darkening and the stars falling. Just as these cosmic signs point to the coming of God's kingdom, Joseph's imprisonment points to a moment when everything will change. Though the light of Joseph's life seems dim, and his future seems uncertain, God is still working behind the scenes to prepare him for the moment when he will rise.

Joseph's trials in Egypt teach us that the tribulations we face are not the end of the story. Just as the **6th Seal** is not the final seal but a precursor to God's judgment and redemption, Joseph's trials are preparing him for a greater role. In the chapters ahead, we will see how Joseph moves from prison to a position of unparalleled power in Egypt, just as God's plan for redemption moves from tribulation to triumph.

As we reflect on Joseph's life thus far, we are reminded that in times of tribulation, our faith and endurance are tested, but they also serve to refine us for greater things. The shaking of our lives is not without purpose; it is part of God's plan to prepare us for His ultimate deliverance.

Chapter 2: Study Questions For Reflection

The Pit and the 6th Seal—Shaken but Not Destroyed:

1. How does Joseph's experience in the pit symbolize the periods of darkness or "shaking" that we encounter in our lives?
2. The 6th Seal speaks of cosmic upheaval. How does this relate to times when your world has been turned upside down? How can faith be sustained through such times?
3. What does Joseph's resilience in the face of betrayal and hardship teach us about enduring faith?
4. How does God prepare us for future purposes during our times of trial, much like He did with Joseph?

CHAPTER 3: FROM PRISON TO POWER —THE ENDURANCE OF THE SAINTS

Joseph's time in prison is a pivotal moment in his story. Stripped of his status and falsely accused, Joseph finds himself in the lowest place imaginable. Yet, as we have seen, this is not the end for him but a period of testing and refinement. His time in prison teaches us much about the nature of tribulation, perseverance, and the preparation for something greater—just as the 6th Seal in Revelation serves as a precursor to God's ultimate plan for redemption.

Prison, in Joseph's case, is not merely a place of punishment; it is a place of waiting. In the Bible, waiting is often synonymous with endurance and faithfulness. The faithful must wait for God's timing, even when their circumstances seem unbearable. For Joseph, this waiting was not passive. He continued to act with integrity, gaining the trust of the prison warden and taking responsibility for the other prisoners. In this way, Joseph's life in prison reflects the call to endurance that the **6th Seal** demands from believers. It is a reminder that even in the midst of suffering, we are called to remain faithful and to trust in God's plan.

In prison, Joseph encounters two of Pharaoh's servants—the chief cupbearer and the chief baker—who have been imprisoned for offenses against their master. Both men have troubling dreams on the same night, and they come to Joseph for interpretation. This moment is significant, for it marks the beginning of Joseph's rise from the depths of the prison to the heights of power in Egypt. His gift of interpreting dreams, first seen in his own youthful visions, is now used to help others. This not only reflects Joseph's growing maturity but also demonstrates how God uses his gifts even in the darkest circumstances.

Joseph listens to the dreams of the cupbearer and the baker. To the cupbearer, Joseph offers good news: in three days, he will be restored to his position in Pharaoh's court. To the baker, however, Joseph reveals that in three days, he will be executed. Both interpretations prove true, and Joseph's reputation as an interpreter of dreams begins to spread. Before the cupbearer is released, Joseph makes one request: that the cupbearer remember him and mention him to Pharaoh, hoping this would be his chance to escape the prison.

But the cupbearer forgets Joseph, and he remains in prison for two more years. This period of continued waiting is perhaps one of the most difficult for Joseph. He has done everything right—he has remained faithful, he has used his gifts, and yet he is still forgotten, still imprisoned. It is here that Joseph's endurance is tested the most. In the same way, believers who live through the events of the **6th Seal** will experience a time of great tribulation, where they too may feel forgotten or abandoned. But Joseph's story reminds us that even when we feel forgotten by the world, God has not forgotten us. His plan is still at work, even if we cannot yet see it.

After two years, Pharaoh himself has a series of troubling dreams. In these dreams, he sees seven fat cows followed by seven gaunt cows, and then seven healthy ears of grain followed by seven withered ears of grain. None of Pharaoh's magicians or wise men can interpret the dreams, and it is only then that the cupbearer remembers Joseph. He tells Pharaoh of the Hebrew prisoner who correctly interpreted his own dream. Joseph is summoned from the prison to Pharaoh's court, and in this moment, his life changes forever.

When Joseph is brought before Pharaoh, he does not claim the ability to interpret the dream for himself. Instead, he humbly acknowledges that the interpretation will come from God. This humility is a testament to Joseph's faith, even after all the trials he has endured. He has not become bitter or proud; instead, he remains steadfast in his trust in God. This humility in the face of power is an important lesson for all believers, especially those who endure trials for the sake of righteousness.

Joseph interprets Pharaoh's dreams with precision. The seven fat cows and the seven healthy ears of grain represent seven years of abundance, while the seven gaunt cows and the seven withered ears represent seven years of severe famine. Joseph not only interprets the dream but also provides a plan of action: during the seven years of plenty, Egypt should store surplus grain so that they will have enough to survive the seven years of famine. Pharaoh, impressed not only by Joseph's wisdom but also by his integrity, appoints him as the second most powerful man in Egypt, placing him in charge of preparing the nation for the coming famine.

This moment marks Joseph's rise from the pit of despair to the pinnacle of power. It is a dramatic reversal of fortune, but it is also the fulfillment of God's plan. Just as the **6th Seal** leads to tribulation before deliverance, Joseph's years of suffering lead to a position where he can save not only Egypt but also his own family. His rise to power is not about personal glory; it is about God's purpose being fulfilled through him.

In this way, Joseph's rise reflects the biblical principle that tribulation prepares us for greater service. The trials he endured were not without purpose—they shaped him into the man who could carry the weight of responsibility that Pharaoh placed upon him. His endurance through unjust suffering mirrors the call to all believers to remain faithful through tribulation, knowing that God is preparing something greater on the other side.

Joseph's journey from the pit to the palace is not just a story of personal triumph but of divine orchestration. His endurance through the darkest of times exemplifies the steadfastness required of all believers. From slavery to imprisonment, Joseph never lost sight of God's sovereignty. This kind of faith—one that holds on through every trial—opens the door for God's extraordinary purposes to be fulfilled. As we prepare to explore Joseph's rise to power, let us remember that our faith, like Joseph's, is often refined through adversity, preparing us for the work God has ahead.

Chapter 3: Study Questions For Reflection

From Prison to Power—The Endurance of the Saints:

1. What parallels do you see between Joseph's unjust imprisonment and the trials believers face as they endure the challenges of life?
2. How does Joseph's integrity and faithfulness in prison inspire you to remain faithful in difficult circumstances?
3. Reflect on a time when you felt forgotten or overlooked. How did God use that period of waiting in your life for His purposes?
4. What does Joseph's rise to power teach us about God's timing and the rewards of perseverance?

CHAPTER 4: MANAGING THE FAMINE—THE WISDOM OF JOSEPH

After his rise to power, Joseph begins the monumental task of managing the abundance and preparing for the coming famine, a task that demonstrates not only his leadership but also his reliance on God's wisdom. This period in Joseph's life reflects the ongoing preparation that believers are called to make in the face of coming trials, just as the Feast of Trumpets is a call to spiritual preparedness.

For seven years, Egypt enjoys unparalleled prosperity, with the land yielding abundant crops. Joseph organizes the collection and storage of grain, ensuring that the nation is well-prepared for the future. The people of Egypt may not fully grasp the significance of Joseph's preparations, just as many do not recognize the urgency of spiritual readiness. However, Joseph's foresight and wisdom, rooted in his ability to interpret Pharaoh's dreams and understand God's plan, make him a model of how to act in times of plenty to prepare for times of trial.

As the famine begins to spread, not only does Egypt benefit

from Joseph's foresight, but so do the surrounding nations. The famine affects all the lands, and people from many nations come to Egypt to buy grain. In this, Joseph's leadership becomes a beacon of hope, just as the faithful are called to be a light to the nations in times of darkness. His ability to manage the crisis with integrity and compassion exemplifies the characteristics of godly leadership—humility, wisdom, and stewardship.

But Joseph's story is not just about managing the physical crisis of famine; it is also a time of personal and spiritual reconciliation. As the famine grows severe, Joseph's own family is drawn into his sphere of influence, though they do not yet know it. His brothers, the very ones who betrayed him years earlier, are forced by desperation to come to Egypt to buy food. In this moment, Joseph stands in a position of power over them, able to exact revenge or offer forgiveness.

When his brothers arrive in Egypt, they do not recognize Joseph, who is now dressed as an Egyptian ruler and speaks through an interpreter. Joseph, however, recognizes them immediately. The years of separation and betrayal come flooding back, but instead of lashing out in anger, Joseph begins a process that will test their hearts and ultimately lead to reconciliation. This part of Joseph's story mirrors the **Feast of Atonement**, which is a time of reflection, repentance, and reconciliation between God and His people.

Joseph's wisdom in storing grain during times of plenty shows not only his practical leadership but also the spiritual foresight that comes from trusting in God's guidance. This wisdom saved nations, illustrating how faith, preparation, and stewardship go hand in hand. Like Joseph, we are called to prepare—both in times of abundance and in times of spiritual dryness. As we navigate the challenges of life, may we seek God's wisdom, trusting that His provision will sustain us, even when we face future "famines." In the next chapter, we will explore how this same wisdom leads Joseph to another essential role in the redemption of his family.

Joseph's rise to power is not just a personal victory, but the beginning of a divine assignment that would save nations from destruction. His ability to organize and manage Egypt's resources during a period of unparalleled abundance is a testimony to his wisdom and reliance on God's guidance. In doing so, Joseph models a principle of preparation that transcends the physical realm: just as he prepared Egypt for the coming famine, we too are called to prepare spiritually for the trials and tribulations we may face in life.

For seven years, the land of Egypt flourished under Joseph's careful management. Yet, the people may not have understood the significance of his actions. Like many in the world today, they likely lived in the moment, unaware of the storm that would eventually arrive. Joseph's foresight, however, was rooted in God's revelation through Pharaoh's dreams. His actions, driven by faith and understanding of God's plan, serve as a reminder to believers that preparation in times of prosperity is crucial for enduring future challenges.

The famine that struck Egypt and the surrounding nations was severe, affecting not only the lives of individuals but entire communities. Joseph's leadership became a beacon of hope, not just for the Egyptians but for people from other nations who came seeking sustenance. His ability to manage a crisis with wisdom and compassion offers a profound lesson in godly leadership—one that blends humility, stewardship, and a commitment to serving others. In this, we see Joseph's role as a type of Christ, a savior figure who provides both physical and spiritual nourishment.

But the famine brought more than just external challenges; it also initiated the process of healing and reconciliation within Joseph's own family. The very brothers who betrayed him now came seeking help, unaware that the powerful figure before them was the one they had once cast aside. In this moment, Joseph's leadership extended beyond managing resources to managing emotions, relationships, and, ultimately, forgiveness.

This period mirrors the heart of the Feast of Atonement—a time of deep reflection, repentance, and reconciliation.

Joseph's wisdom was not just in storing grain, but in allowing time for the hearts of his brothers to be tested and transformed. His actions demonstrate that true reconciliation requires both a recognition of wrongs and a willingness to forgive. He could have easily used his power to exact revenge, but instead, Joseph chose a path that honored God's plan for restoration. In this way, Joseph's story becomes a profound lesson in both the preparation required for physical survival and the spiritual readiness needed for reconciliation and redemption.

As we reflect on Joseph's leadership, we are reminded that preparation, whether for a physical famine or a spiritual trial, is essential. Joseph's example calls us to be diligent in seasons of abundance, knowing that difficult times may lie ahead. Just as he prepared Egypt for famine, we too must store up spiritual strength through faith, prayer, and obedience, trusting in God's provision for whatever lies ahead.

In the next chapter, we will see how this same wisdom and divine foresight lead Joseph to a crucial role in the redemption and reconciliation of his family. His story will continue to unfold, offering deeper insights into God's ultimate plan for His people—a plan that blends endurance, preparation, and grace in the face of adversity.

Chapter 4: Study Questions For Reflection

Managing the Famine—The Wisdom of Joseph:

1. How did Joseph's foresight and wisdom in managing the famine reflect God's provision in times of crisis?
2. What lessons can we learn from Joseph's leadership in preparation and stewardship during the years of abundance and famine?
3. In your own life, how do you respond to times of abundance? What steps can you take to ensure that you are prepared for future challenges, both physically and spiritually?
4. Joseph's ability to provide for not only Egypt but also surrounding nations demonstrated his role as a wise leader. How can we apply principles of generosity and wise resource management in our daily lives?
5. How does Joseph's wisdom in managing the famine show us the importance of trusting in God's guidance, even in the face of overwhelming challenges?

CHAPTER 5: THE FEAST OF ATONEMENT—FORGIVENESS AND RECONCILIATION

Joseph's interactions with his brothers offer one of the clearest biblical examples of reconciliation, a concept central to the Feast of Atonement. This sacred time, observed annually by the Israelites, was marked by deep repentance and the desire to restore broken relationships—both between individuals and with God. As Joseph stands before the brothers who sold him into slavery, he becomes a living reflection of atonement, where old sins are confronted, forgiveness is extended, and relationships are restored.

In this moment, the power dynamic has dramatically shifted. Years earlier, Joseph was at the mercy of his brothers' jealousy and hatred. But now, they are the ones standing in need of mercy. They come to Egypt seeking food, unaware that the brother they betrayed now holds their fate in his hands. Joseph recognizes his brothers immediately, yet chooses to remain anonymous to them, initiating a process of testing and repentance that will lead to full restoration—but only after the hearts of his brothers are revealed.

Joseph's first test is to accuse his brothers of being spies. He holds them in custody for three days—a period reminiscent of waiting, reflection, and spiritual awakening. On the third day, Joseph releases them but demands that they bring their youngest brother, Benjamin, as proof of their innocence. This demand triggers profound guilt in the brothers. They are forced to confront their past, with their minds drawn back to the fateful day when they sold Joseph into slavery. "We are being punished because of our brother," they confess to one another, acknowledging for the first time their wrongdoing.

This period of self-reflection is crucial. Just as the Feast of Atonement requires individuals to reflect deeply on their sins and seek reconciliation, Joseph's brothers must face the weight of their past actions. This is no superficial acknowledgment; it is the beginning of genuine repentance. The gravity of their sin is not lost on them as they believe they are being judged for the betrayal of their brother. However, what they do not realize is that the path toward forgiveness has already begun, guided by Joseph's deliberate actions to draw out their hearts.

Upon their return to Canaan, the brothers relay Joseph's demands to their father, Jacob. Jacob's reaction is one of deep sorrow and fear. Having already lost Joseph, he cannot bear the thought of losing Benjamin, the last remaining son of his beloved wife, Rachel. However, as the famine intensifies, Jacob's hand is forced. He reluctantly agrees to send Benjamin with his brothers back to Egypt, entrusting the lives of his children into the hands of God, a step of faith amidst his overwhelming fear.

When the brothers return to Egypt with Benjamin, Joseph's testing continues. He arranges a feast for them, showing unexpected kindness, but secretly he places his silver cup in Benjamin's sack. The symbolism of this cup—often associated with royalty, divination, or judgment—adds weight to the unfolding drama. After the brothers depart, Joseph's steward pursues them, accusing them of theft. This dramatic moment mirrors their earlier betrayal of Joseph, as they once again face a situation where they could easily sacrifice one brother to save themselves.

In this climactic moment, the ultimate test of character is revealed. Will the brothers repeat their past mistake, allowing Benjamin to be enslaved while they return home in peace? Judah, the brother who once suggested selling Joseph into slavery, steps forward with a remarkable act of self-sacrifice. He pleads for Benjamin's release and offers himself as a substitute, declaring that their father would not survive losing another son. This act of intercession marks a profound change in Judah and the brothers as a whole. No longer driven by selfishness and jealousy, they have become willing to sacrifice themselves for the sake of their family.

Judah's selflessness is a critical turning point. It demonstrates true repentance, the kind of repentance that leads to reconciliation. Joseph, upon witnessing this transformation, can no longer maintain his hidden identity. Overcome with emotion, he reveals himself to his brothers, declaring, "I am Joseph, your brother, whom you sold into Egypt!" The shock and terror that grip his brothers in this moment is palpable. They fear not only his power but also the justice they believe they deserve for their actions. Surely Joseph, now in a position of ultimate authority, will exact revenge for the evil they committed against him.

Yet Joseph's response is one of grace and forgiveness, perhaps one of the most profound examples of forgiveness in Scripture. Rather than condemning his brothers, he offers them peace, saying, "Do not be distressed or angry with yourselves because you sold me here, for God sent me before you to preserve life" (Genesis 45:5). This statement encapsulates Joseph's deep understanding of God's sovereignty. He sees beyond the actions of his brothers, recognizing that while they intended harm, God had used their betrayal to bring about a greater purpose—the salvation of many.

This moment of forgiveness is a powerful reflection of the Feast of Atonement. Just as the Israelites sought forgiveness from God and one another during this holy day, Joseph extends forgiveness to his brothers, not holding their sins against them but instead choosing reconciliation. His perspective on their betrayal—seeing it as part of God's plan—enables him to release any bitterness or desire for revenge. In this, Joseph models the heart of atonement: the restoration of relationships through forgiveness and divine grace.

Joseph's actions also echo the greater narrative of Christ's atonement. Like Joseph, Christ was betrayed by those closest to Him, yet He chose to forgive rather than condemn. Just as Joseph's forgiveness preserved the lives of his family and many others, Christ's forgiveness through the cross brings life and reconciliation to all who believe. Both Joseph and Christ show that forgiveness is not a denial of wrongdoing but an acknowledgment that God's grace is greater than our sins.

As we reflect on this story, we are reminded of the power of forgiveness to transform lives and restore what was once broken. Joseph's forgiveness of his brothers teaches us that true reconciliation requires both parties to seek restoration. His brothers had to come to a place of repentance, and Joseph had to be willing to forgive. This delicate balance is what makes reconciliation possible, both in our relationships with others and in our relationship with God.

The story of Joseph and his brothers is a timeless reminder that God is always at work to reconcile us to Himself, no matter the depth of our sins. Through repentance and forgiveness, healing is possible, and relationships can be restored. Just as Joseph's family was brought back together, we too are invited to experience the joy of reconciliation with God and with those around us.

As we consider our own relationships, may we be reminded that the path to forgiveness often leads us back to the heart of God, where true atonement is found. Whether we need to forgive or seek forgiveness, Joseph's story encourages us to trust in God's sovereign plan, knowing that He can bring restoration even from the most painful of circumstances.

Chapter 5: Study Questions For Reflection

The Feast of Atonement—Forgiveness and Reconciliation:

1. How does Joseph's decision to forgive his brothers reflect the spirit of the Feast of Atonement, which focuses on repentance and reconciliation with God?

2. In what ways does Joseph test his brothers' hearts before fully reconciling with them? What does this teach us about the process of genuine reconciliation?

3. Reflect on a time when you were in need of forgiveness or when you extended forgiveness to someone else. How did the process of reconciliation impact you or the other person involved?

4. What role does humility play in both giving and receiving forgiveness, as seen in the interactions between Joseph and his brothers?

5. How can we apply Joseph's example of grace and forgiveness to relationships in our own lives, particularly in situations where we have been deeply hurt or betrayed?

6. The Feast of Atonement is about restoring relationships with God and with others. How can you seek to reconcile broken relationships in your life and draw closer to God in the process?

CHAPTER 6: RESTORATION OF THE FAMILY—THE SPIRITUAL TEMPLE

The reconciliation of Joseph's family is one of the most profound moments in Scripture, not only because it resolves years of separation and pain but because it serves as a symbol of the greater reconciliation that God offers to all His people. Joseph's personal journey of suffering, endurance, and eventual triumph is the backdrop for the ultimate act of restoration: the healing of his family. But this event goes beyond a simple familial reunion; it is rich with spiritual meaning, pointing to God's covenantal promises and His redemptive plan for humanity.

Joseph's story reaches its emotional climax when Jacob, now an old man, learns that his beloved son is alive. The grief that had weighed on Jacob's heart for years lifts in an instant. For so long, he had believed that his favorite son had been torn apart by wild animals, lost forever. The news that Joseph is not only alive but flourishing in Egypt is almost too good to be true. Joseph's invitation to his family to come and live in Egypt during the famine is more than a gesture of generosity; it is a picture of God's invitation to His people to dwell with Him, even in the midst of trials and suffering. Just as Joseph provides for his family during a time of global crisis, so God provides for His people, offering sustenance, shelter, and restoration in times of hardship.

Jacob's decision to move his entire household to Egypt is a pivotal moment, both for his family and for the unfolding story of God's people. The twelve sons of Jacob represent the twelve tribes of Israel, and their relocation to Egypt sets the stage for the future Exodus and the birth of the nation of Israel. What began as a personal story of betrayal and reconciliation now takes on a national and prophetic significance. Joseph's role in saving his family is not just about preserving a family line—it is about preserving God's covenant promises to Abraham, Isaac, and Jacob. Through Joseph's actions, God is ensuring the survival of the chosen people, from whom the Messiah will eventually come.

As Jacob and his family make their way to Egypt, there is a sense that this is not merely a journey of physical relocation but a journey of spiritual significance. In many ways, the move to Egypt mirrors the spiritual journey that all believers undertake. Just as Jacob had to trust in God's provision and guidance, so too are we called to trust God as we navigate the uncertainties of life. The journey to Egypt is not without its risks, yet Jacob moves forward in faith, confident that God's promises will be fulfilled, even in a foreign land.

When Jacob and Joseph finally reunite, the scene is filled with poignant emotion. Jacob, who for so long believed his son was dead, is now able to embrace him once again. It is a moment of complete restoration, not only of father and son but of the entire family. This reunion is a powerful image of the reconciliation that the Feast of Atonement points to—a time when broken relationships are healed, and estranged individuals are brought back into fellowship. Just as Jacob's heart is restored by seeing his son again, so too does God seek to restore His relationship with humanity, offering forgiveness and reconciliation through the atoning work of Christ.

The spiritual significance of Joseph's reunion with his family cannot be overstated. Throughout Scripture, God's desire is to reconcile and restore, and Joseph's story is a living example of that divine plan. His forgiveness of his brothers, his provision for his family, and his willingness to be the means of their salvation are all reflections of God's character. In Joseph, we see a type of Christ—a savior figure who endures suffering, overcomes betrayal, and ultimately offers life and salvation to those who rejected him. Just as Joseph provides for his family, Christ provides for His people, offering spiritual sustenance and eternal life.

Joseph's story, however, is not just about reconciliation on a personal level. It also foreshadows the future establishment of Israel as a nation. The twelve sons of Jacob, who are now reunited in Egypt, will go on to form the twelve tribes of Israel. In this way, the reconciliation of Joseph's family is not just the restoration of a household but the beginning of the fulfillment of God's covenant promises to Abraham, Isaac, and Jacob. Through Joseph's leadership and provision, the family is preserved, and the foundation for the future nation of Israel is laid. This moment is a critical turning point in redemptive history, as it sets the stage for the eventual Exodus, where God will deliver His people from Egypt and establish them as a nation.

As we reflect on this restoration of Joseph's family, it is important to recognize that their reconciliation is a foreshadowing of the greater spiritual restoration that Christ brings to humanity. The brokenness that once divided Joseph from his brothers mirrors the division between God and His people, a division that would one day be mended by the ultimate sacrifice of Christ. Just as Joseph's reunion with his family points to God's redemptive work, our lives too are being built into a spiritual temple, with Christ as the cornerstone. In Ephesians

2:19-22, Paul speaks of believers being "fellow citizens with the saints and members of the household of God," built on the foundation of the apostles and prophets, with Jesus Christ as the cornerstone. This spiritual temple, made up of all who believe in Christ, is the ultimate fulfillment of God's desire to dwell with His people.

The concept of the spiritual temple is one that runs throughout Scripture, from the tabernacle in the wilderness to the temple in Jerusalem, and ultimately to the church, the body of believers, who are being built up into a dwelling place for God. Joseph's story, with its themes of reconciliation and restoration, points forward to this spiritual reality. Just as Joseph's family was restored and brought together, so too are we being restored and united in Christ. The division caused by sin is being healed, and we are being built into a spiritual house, where God's presence dwells.

As we conclude this exploration of Joseph's life, it becomes clear that his story is far more than a personal journey of triumph over adversity. It is a prophetic type, pointing to the 6th Seal, the Feast of Trumpets, and the Feast of Atonement. Through his trials, Joseph teaches us about endurance, faith, and the sovereign hand of God at work even in the darkest moments. Through his leadership, he shows us the importance of preparation and stewardship. And through his forgiveness, Joseph reflects the heart of God, who desires reconciliation and restoration with His people.

The restoration of Joseph's family is a profound picture of the restoration that Christ offers to all who come to Him. Just as Joseph provided for his family during the famine, Christ provides for us in our times of spiritual need. Just as Joseph forgave those who betrayed him, Christ forgives us and invites us into a restored relationship with God. And just as Joseph's family was preserved in Egypt, so too are we preserved in Christ, who sustains us through every trial and tribulation.

As we look ahead to the final chapters of history, let us reflect on the ways God is restoring us—both individually and corporately—into His spiritual family. The reconciliation of Joseph's family is a reminder that no matter how deep the division, no matter how long the separation, God is always at work to restore, heal, and bring us back into fellowship with Him. Just as Joseph's brothers were brought to a place of repentance and reconciliation, so too are we invited to experience the joy of being reconciled to God through Christ.

In this way, Joseph's story continues to speak to us today, offering hope, encouragement, and a powerful reminder of God's unfailing love and His desire to dwell with His people. Through the restoration of Joseph's family, we see a glimpse of the ultimate restoration that awaits all who put their trust in Christ—the restoration of all things, where sin and death will be no more, and we will dwell with God in perfect harmony for eternity.

Chapter 6: Study Questions For Reflection

Restoration of the Family—The Spiritual Temple:

1. How does Joseph's restoration of his family reflect God's desire to restore broken relationships with His people?

2. What role does forgiveness and grace play in the healing of Joseph's family? How can you apply these principles to relationships in your life?

3. The restoration of Joseph's family came after a period of suffering and separation. In what ways have you experienced restoration in your life after a season of trial?

4. Joseph's family represented the foundation of the twelve tribes of Israel. How does this restoration foreshadow the spiritual restoration that Christ offers through His sacrifice?

5. In what ways do you see the concept of a "spiritual temple" reflected in your own life? How are you allowing God to restore and build you up as a spiritual house?

6. How does Joseph's reunion with his father, Jacob, serve as a model for the ultimate reunion between God and His people? What can we learn from this reunion about God's heart for reconciliation and restoration?

CHAPTER 7: JOSEPH—A LIFE OF ENDURANCE, PREPARATION, AND RECONCILIATION

Joseph's life is one of the most profound narratives in Scripture, not simply because of his personal triumphs but because of the deep spiritual truths it conveys. His story, spanning from betrayal to reconciliation, from slavery to sovereignty, offers a blueprint for how to navigate life's greatest challenges with faith, wisdom, and humility. Through Joseph's journey, we see the hand of God at work, even in the darkest moments, guiding him toward his ultimate purpose. In the narrative of Joseph, we find enduring lessons of faith, preparation, and reconciliation—principles that speak not only to his time but resonate deeply in our lives today.

Joseph's life begins with great promise. As the favored son of Jacob, Joseph is gifted with a beautiful coat, a symbol of his father's love and a sign of the destiny that lies ahead. However, this favor comes at a cost. His brothers' jealousy festers into hatred, and Joseph's life takes a drastic turn when they sell him into slavery. The betrayal of his brothers mirrors the betrayal that all of humanity has experienced at various points in life, whether through personal relationships or the brokenness of the world. Yet, Joseph's response to this betrayal is not one of bitterness or despair. Instead, he begins a journey of endurance, trusting in God's promises even when the circumstances seem to point in the opposite direction.

Endurance Through Trials

The theme of endurance is woven throughout Joseph's story. After being sold into slavery, Joseph finds himself in Egypt, working in the house of Potiphar. Despite the injustice he has suffered, Joseph does not give in to self-pity or resentment. Instead, he excels in his work, gaining the trust of Potiphar and rising to a position of authority within the household. This period of Joseph's life reflects the importance of remaining faithful in small things, even when larger promises seem distant. It is in these moments of quiet faithfulness that God often prepares us for greater things.

However, Joseph's endurance is tested once again when he is falsely accused by Potiphar's wife and thrown into prison. This second betrayal could have easily broken his spirit, but Joseph remains steadfast. In the prison, he once again rises to a position of leadership, interpreting the dreams of his fellow prisoners with accuracy and grace. These moments of interpreting dreams are not just acts of service; they are glimpses of the divine calling that remains on Joseph's life. Even in the pit of despair, Joseph's faith in God's plan remains unshaken. His ability to endure through these trials is a testimony to the strength of his character and his unwavering trust in God's faithfulness.

Joseph's endurance teaches us that trials are not meaningless, but rather are part of God's larger plan for our lives. Just as Joseph's time in prison prepared him for the responsibilities that lay ahead, the difficulties we face today may be preparing us for the future roles God has in store for us. Endurance in the face of adversity shapes us, refines our character, and draws us closer to God. It is through the fires of affliction that we are molded into the people God has called us to be.

Preparation For The Future

The theme of preparation is closely tied to endurance in Joseph's life. His ability to interpret dreams not only provides insight into the present but also allows him to prepare for the future. This gift, which first appears in his youth when he dreams of his brothers bowing down to him, becomes the key to his rise to power in Egypt. When Pharaoh is troubled by dreams of seven years of plenty followed by seven years of famine, it is Joseph who, through divine revelation, provides both the interpretation and the solution.

Joseph's preparation for the future is both practical and spiritual. On a practical level, he organizes the storage of grain during the years of abundance, ensuring that Egypt will have enough food to survive the coming famine. This act of stewardship is a model of wise leadership, showing the importance of planning and foresight. But Joseph's preparation is also spiritual. His ability to see beyond the present circumstances and trust in God's guidance allows him to act with confidence and wisdom. He is not merely responding to the immediate crisis; he is preparing for the future, trusting that God's plan will unfold in His perfect timing.

In our own lives, we are called to prepare in similar ways. Just as Joseph stored up grain during the years of plenty, we are called to store up spiritual resources during seasons of abundance, so that we are ready when trials come. This preparation involves nurturing our relationship with God through prayer, study of Scripture, and community with other believers. It also involves stewarding the gifts and resources God has given us, so that we can be a blessing to others in times of need. Joseph's life reminds us that preparation is not just about survival; it is about thriving in the midst of adversity, trusting that God's provision is always sufficient.

Reconciliation And Forgiveness

At the heart of Joseph's story, however, is reconciliation. The reunion with his family, and the forgiveness he extends to his brothers, is one of the most powerful images of reconciliation in Scripture. After years of separation and betrayal, Joseph stands before the very brothers who sold him into slavery, not with anger or revenge, but with grace and forgiveness. His ability to forgive those who wronged him is a reflection of God's own heart of reconciliation toward humanity.

Joseph's brothers, who once acted out of jealousy and hatred, are now in a position of vulnerability. They come to Egypt seeking food during the famine, unaware that the man who stands before them is the brother they betrayed. When Joseph reveals his identity, they are filled with fear, expecting him to exact revenge. But instead of retribution, Joseph offers forgiveness, saying, "Do not be distressed or angry with yourselves because you sold me here, for God sent me before you to preserve life" (Genesis 45:5).

This moment of forgiveness is a profound reflection of God's desire to reconcile with His people. Just as Joseph was willing to forgive those who betrayed him, God is willing to forgive us—restoring not just individual relationships but bringing us back into communion with Him. Joseph's forgiveness is rooted in his deep understanding of God's sovereignty. He recognizes that what his brothers meant for evil, God used for good. This recognition allows Joseph to offer grace instead of judgment, just as Christ offers forgiveness to those who repent and seek reconciliation.

In Joseph, we see a type of Christ, offering reconciliation to those who would otherwise be lost. His forgiveness of his brothers mirrors Christ's forgiveness of sinners, inviting us into restored relationship with God. This act of reconciliation is not just about personal healing; it is about participating in God's redemptive plan for the world. Just as Joseph's forgiveness restored his family, Christ's forgiveness restores humanity, bringing us back into fellowship with the Father.

A Spiritual Blueprint

As we conclude this study of Joseph's life and its connection to the prophetic themes in Scripture, we are left with the understanding that Joseph's story is not just a historical account, but a spiritual blueprint. It shows us how to endure suffering, how to prepare for both the challenges and blessings ahead, and how to pursue reconciliation—with God, with others, and with ourselves.

Joseph's life teaches us that endurance through trials is not only possible but necessary for spiritual growth. His ability to remain faithful in the face of injustice and hardship reminds us that God is always at work, even when we cannot see it. Like Joseph, we are called to trust in God's promises, even when the path before us seems uncertain.

His life also teaches us the importance of preparation. Joseph's wisdom in preparing for the famine serves as a model for how we should approach both physical and spiritual challenges. By storing up resources in times of plenty, Joseph ensured the survival of his family and the nation of Egypt. In the same way, we are called to prepare for the future by investing in our spiritual lives, trusting that God will provide for us in times of need.

Finally, Joseph's story is a powerful reminder of the importance of reconciliation. His willingness to forgive his brothers and restore his family reflects the heart of God, who desires reconciliation with His people. In Joseph's life, we see a reflection of Christ, who offers forgiveness and reconciliation to all who come to Him.

In doing so, we participate in God's redemptive plan, allowing Him to shape us into vessels of His grace, wisdom, and love. Like Joseph, we are called to endure, to prepare, and to forgive, trusting that God's sovereign plan is always at work, even in the darkest moments. As we walk this path, may we, like Joseph, be a light to the world, offering hope, forgiveness, and reconciliation to all who seek it.

Chapter 7: Study Questions For Reflection

Joseph—A Life of Endurance, Preparation, and Reconciliation:

1. Looking back on Joseph's journey, how can you apply the lessons of endurance through trials to your own life? In what areas is God calling you to trust in His timing?

2. How did Joseph's preparation during times of abundance help him and others survive the famine? What practical steps can you take today to prepare spiritually and physically for future challenges?

3. Joseph's life is a story of reconciliation, both with his family and with God's larger redemptive plan. How can you seek reconciliation in relationships where there is division or pain?

4. In what ways has God shaped your character through trials, much like He did with Joseph? How can you continue to grow in faith during seasons of waiting or hardship?

5. Joseph's faithfulness in every circumstance—from the pit to the palace—demonstrates unwavering trust in God's providence. How can you cultivate a similar trust in God's plan for your life, even when the path is unclear?

6. Reflect on the themes of endurance, preparation, and reconciliation. Which of these themes resonates most with you in your current season of life, and how can you allow God to work through it?

CHAPTER 8: REFLECTING ON JOSEPH'S LIFE AND TRIALS—A FORESHADOWING OF THE 6TH SEAL

As we conclude our exploration of Joseph's life, it becomes clear that his journey is far more than just a personal narrative of suffering and triumph. Joseph's trials, from his betrayal by his brothers to his rise as the ruler of Egypt, reflect spiritual truths that transcend time. His life mirrors the broader themes of tribulation, endurance, and redemption that are central to Scripture, and in particular, his journey foreshadows the prophetic events described in the 6th Seal of the Book of Revelation. In Joseph's life, we see a pattern that points toward the cosmic shaking of the last days, a period when the world will be tested, and God's ultimate plan for humanity will be revealed.

The 6th Seal, as described in Revelation 6:12-17, speaks of a time of great upheaval—earthquakes, the darkening of the sun, the moon turning to blood, and stars falling from the sky. It is a moment when the foundations of the world are shaken, and people cry out in fear of God's judgment. Though this prophecy describes a future event, its themes of tribulation and divine intervention can be seen reflected in Joseph's life. Joseph's personal world was shaken to its core when he was sold into slavery, betrayed by those closest to him, and imprisoned unjustly. Yet, like the 6th Seal, Joseph's trials were not the end of his story but the beginning of God's redemptive work in his life and the lives of those around him.

Joseph's Life As A Microcosm Of The 6Th Seal

Joseph's journey can be viewed as a microcosm of the cosmic events described in the 6th Seal. His life begins in a place of favor and security, much like the stability of the world before the opening of the seals in Revelation. Joseph is the favored son of Jacob, clothed in a richly ornamented robe, and set apart for a special purpose. However, this favor leads to jealousy and betrayal, much like how the world, in its comfort and complacency, will be jolted by the events of the 6th Seal. The betrayal Joseph experiences at the hands of his brothers is a personal reflection of the larger betrayals and divisions that will mark the end times.

Joseph's fall into slavery and imprisonment represents the personal tribulation that foreshadows the collective tribulation of the world. His life is shattered, just as the world will be shaken during the 6th Seal. Yet, in the midst of his suffering, Joseph remains faithful, trusting in God's plan even when the future seems uncertain. This endurance through suffering reflects the call for believers to remain steadfast during the trials that are to come. Just as Joseph's personal tribulation led to his eventual exaltation, so too will the tribulation of the 6th Seal lead to the revelation of God's sovereignty and the ultimate triumph of His kingdom.

In both Joseph's story and the 6th Seal, there is a pattern of judgment followed by deliverance. For Joseph, his unjust imprisonment was a time of testing, but it ultimately became the means by which God elevated him to a position of authority. Similarly, the 6th Seal represents a time of cosmic judgment, but it is not the final word. Instead, it is a precursor to the coming of God's kingdom and the redemption of His people. Just as Joseph's rise to power brought salvation to Egypt and his family, the events of the 6th Seal will lead to the salvation of the faithful and the establishment of God's reign on earth.

Endurance And Faithfulness Amidst Tribulation

One of the key themes of Joseph's life is endurance—remaining faithful to God's promises even in the face of overwhelming adversity. This endurance is a crucial lesson for believers as we consider the trials of the 6th Seal. Joseph's journey was marked by long periods of waiting and uncertainty. After being sold into slavery, he endured years of hardship in Egypt, first as a slave in Potiphar's house and then as a prisoner, falsely accused of a crime he did not commit. During this time, Joseph had no assurance of when or how his circumstances would change. Yet he remained faithful, trusting that God's plan was unfolding, even if he could not see it.

This theme of endurance is echoed in the prophetic description of the 6th Seal. The world will undergo a period of great tribulation, a time when it seems as though everything is falling apart. The very foundations of the earth will be shaken, and people will be gripped by fear. However, just as Joseph's suffering was a precursor to his elevation, the tribulations of the 6th Seal are part of God's plan to bring about His ultimate victory. Believers are called to endure through these trials, trusting that God is in control and that He will bring about deliverance in His time.

Joseph's faithfulness during his trials also highlights the importance of preparation. Even in the midst of his suffering, Joseph was being prepared for the role that God had destined for him. His time in Potiphar's house and in prison were not wasted years; they were formative periods where Joseph's character was refined, and his leadership skills were developed. In the same way, the trials of the 6th Seal are not arbitrary; they serve a purpose in preparing God's people for the fulfillment of His promises. Endurance through suffering is not passive resignation but an active trust in God's redemptive work, even in the midst of tribulation.

Preparation For Deliverance And Redemption

Joseph's life also teaches us the importance of preparation in the face of coming trials. After being elevated to a position of power in Egypt, Joseph's first act was to prepare the nation for the coming famine. Through divine revelation, Joseph knew that seven years of plenty would be followed by seven years of scarcity. Rather than becoming complacent in the years of abundance, Joseph used that time to store up grain and prepare for the hardship that lay ahead. His wisdom in preparing during the good times ensured the survival of Egypt and the surrounding nations during the famine.

This principle of preparation is equally important as we consider the events of the 6th Seal. Just as Joseph prepared for the coming famine, believers are called to prepare for the trials that are to come. The 6th Seal represents a time of cosmic shaking, but it is not a time to be caught off guard. Scripture repeatedly calls believers to be watchful and ready for the return of Christ and the fulfillment of God's kingdom. This preparation is not just about physical survival but about spiritual readiness —cultivating a deep relationship with God, storing up the treasures of faith, and standing firm in the promises of God.

Joseph's role in preparing Egypt for the famine also points

to the greater spiritual preparation that believers are called to undertake. The events of the 6th Seal will be a time of testing, not just for the world but for the people of God. It will be a period that separates those who are grounded in their faith from those who are shaken by fear. Just as Joseph's foresight and wisdom saved many lives, the spiritual preparedness of believers will enable them to stand firm during the tribulation, trusting in God's deliverance.

Reconciliation And Redemption In The End Times

At the heart of Joseph's story is the theme of reconciliation, which finds its ultimate fulfillment in God's plan for humanity. After years of separation and estrangement, Joseph is reunited with his brothers, not in anger or revenge, but in forgiveness and restoration. His willingness to forgive those who wronged him and to reconcile with his family reflects the heart of God, who desires to reconcile humanity to Himself. This theme of reconciliation is central to the events of the 6th Seal and the broader scope of God's redemptive plan.

The 6th Seal, though marked by cosmic upheaval, is ultimately part of God's plan to bring about the reconciliation of all things. Just as Joseph's suffering was a precursor to the restoration of his family, the tribulations of the 6th Seal are a precursor to the restoration of creation. In both cases, suffering serves a purpose —it is a means by which God brings about redemption and reconciliation. The shaking of the heavens and the earth during the 6th Seal is not an act of destruction but an act of renewal, a preparation for the new creation that God will bring forth.

Joseph's story, with its themes of endurance, preparation, and reconciliation, serves as a powerful foreshadowing of the events described in the 6th Seal. His life teaches us that tribulation is not the end of the story; it is the means by which God brings about His greater purposes. Just as Joseph's suffering led to the salvation of his family and the preservation of a nation, the tribulations of the 6th Seal will lead to the ultimate redemption of God's people and the establishment of His kingdom on earth.

Joseph's Role As A Prophetic Type

As we move forward in our study, we will see how Joseph's life not only foreshadows the 6th Seal but also connects to the prophetic themes of the Jewish feasts—particularly the Feast of Trumpets and the Feast of Atonement. These sacred times of preparation, judgment, and reconciliation point us toward the end-time fulfillment of God's promises. Joseph's life, much like these feasts, serves as a reminder of the cycles of preparation, judgment, and ultimate reconciliation that are at the heart of God's redemptive plan. Through his trials, Joseph stands as a prophetic type, offering us a glimpse of the greater realities that are yet to come.

Chapter 8: Study Questions For Reflection

Reflecting on Joseph's Life and Trials—A Foreshadowing of the 6th Seal:

1. **How does Joseph's personal journey of betrayal, suffering, and redemption foreshadow the events described in the 6th Seal?**
   - In what ways do you see parallels between Joseph's trials and the cosmic upheaval of the 6th Seal in Revelation?

2. **Joseph's endurance through tribulation is a central theme in his story. How can Joseph's example of faithfulness inspire us to endure during times of spiritual testing or hardship?**
   - What lessons can we learn from Joseph's ability to trust in God's plan, even when it seemed that everything was falling apart?

3. **In both Joseph's life and the 6th Seal, we see moments of great shaking that lead to a greater purpose. How can we find hope in the idea that God uses times of upheaval to bring about His divine plan?**
   - Have there been times in your life when what seemed like destruction or loss was later revealed to be part of God's greater plan?

4. **Joseph's trials were a form of preparation for his eventual rise to power. How can we, as believers, prepare for the tribulations described in the 6th Seal?**
   - In what ways can we strengthen our faith and reliance on God to be ready for both physical and spiritual trials?

5. **The theme of reconciliation is central to both Joseph's story and God's ultimate plan for humanity. How does Joseph's reconciliation with his brothers reflect**

God's desire to reconcile with His people through Christ?
- What steps can we take to foster reconciliation in our relationships with others, and how does this reflect God's redemptive work?

6. **As we reflect on Joseph's story as a foreshadowing of the 6th Seal, how does this help us understand the nature of suffering and God's sovereignty?**
   - How does knowing that God is present and at work during times of tribulation provide comfort and hope?

PART 2: JOSEPH AND THE FEASTS—PROPHETIC INSIGHTS FROM THE FEAST OF TRUMPETS AND ATONEMENT

CHAPTER 9: JOSEPH'S JOURNEY FROM SUFFERING TO SOVEREIGNTY

Joseph's story is one of the most compelling and intricate narratives in Scripture. From the very beginning, it seems Joseph is marked by God for a special purpose, but the path to that purpose is anything but smooth. His life is filled with moments of great pain and betrayal, yet it is also a story of redemption and restoration, where the hidden hand of God can be seen weaving through every trial and triumph.

Joseph's journey, from being sold into slavery by his brothers to becoming the second-most powerful man in Egypt, is a remarkable demonstration of how God's providence operates, even when it is obscured by suffering. His story is one of divine sovereignty, endurance, and ultimate restoration—a reflection of the greater story God is telling throughout human history.

The Favored Son, The Hated Brother

Joseph's early life is marked by favor, but this favor comes with its own challenges. As the son of Jacob's old age and the firstborn of Rachel, Jacob's beloved wife, Joseph occupies a special place in his father's heart. Jacob's open display of favoritism toward Joseph, symbolized by the "coat of many colors" (Genesis 37:3), stirs resentment among his brothers. This favoritism sets the stage for the deep familial conflict that will soon unfold.

The relationship between Joseph and his brothers is strained even further by Joseph's prophetic dreams. In these dreams, Joseph sees his brothers bowing down to him, a vision that hints at his future rise to power. But instead of viewing these dreams as revelations from God, Joseph's brothers see them as a sign of arrogance. The idea that their younger brother would one day rule over them is unbearable to their pride. Their jealousy festers until it boils over into hatred.

The tension in Joseph's family mirrors the dynamics that play out in many of our own lives. Favoritism, jealousy, and rivalry are common experiences, but Joseph's story reminds us that God's plan is often at work even in the midst of human dysfunction. From the very beginning, Joseph's life is marked by tension between the vision God has given him and the reality of his circumstances—a tension that will follow him throughout his journey.

Betrayed And Sold Into Slavery

Joseph's brothers, unable to bear the thought of his dreams coming true, conspire against him. One day, when Joseph is sent by his father to check on his brothers in the fields, they seize the opportunity to rid themselves of him. They strip him of his coat, throw him into a pit, and contemplate leaving him for dead. But instead of killing him, they decide to sell him to a passing caravan of Ishmaelites, who are heading to Egypt.

This moment of betrayal is a turning point in Joseph's life. In an instant, he goes from being the favored son to a slave in a foreign land. The betrayal of his brothers is not just a familial conflict—it is a deeply personal wound. Joseph's dreams of greatness seem shattered, and his future is now uncertain. What was once a life of security and favor is now marked by slavery and hardship.

Yet, even in this moment of darkness, God's hand is at work. Joseph's sale into slavery is not the end of his story—it is the beginning of a journey that will ultimately lead to his exaltation. This pattern of suffering leading to glory is a common theme in Scripture, and Joseph's life serves as a powerful example of how God can take what was meant for evil and turn it for good.

For us, Joseph's betrayal and sale into slavery serve as a reminder that our own moments of suffering and betrayal are not without purpose. God's plan often unfolds in ways we cannot understand in the moment, but His sovereignty ensures that even our darkest moments can be redeemed for His glory.

A Slave In Egypt: Faithfulness In The Face Of Injustice

Joseph's journey takes him to Egypt, where he is sold to Potiphar, a high-ranking official in Pharaoh's court. Despite the trauma of his betrayal and the loss of his freedom, Joseph chooses to remain faithful. Instead of becoming bitter or resentful, he throws himself into his work, and soon Potiphar recognizes that the Lord is with Joseph, blessing everything he does. As a result, Potiphar puts Joseph in charge of his entire household.

Joseph's rise in Potiphar's household is a testament to his character and faith. Despite his circumstances, he remains faithful to God and to the tasks before him. This is not a passive resignation to fate, but an active trust in God's plan. Joseph's faithfulness in small things leads to greater responsibility, and even in the midst of his suffering, God's favor is evident.

But Joseph's integrity soon leads to another trial. Potiphar's wife, attracted to Joseph, tries to seduce him. When Joseph refuses her advances, she falsely accuses him of attempting to assault her. As a result, Joseph is thrown into prison, even though he has done nothing wrong. This moment of injustice is another turning point in Joseph's life. Once again, he finds himself at the mercy of forces beyond his control, suffering for doing what is right.

In many ways, Joseph's experience in Potiphar's house mirrors the experiences of those who seek to live faithfully in a world that is often unjust. His story reminds us that doing the right thing does not always lead to immediate rewards. In fact, it often leads to more suffering. But Joseph's response to this injustice is a model for us. He does not waver in his faith or give in to despair. Instead, he continues to trust in God, even in the face of false accusations and imprisonment.

In The Prison: Endurance In The Midst Of Trials

Joseph's time in prison is a period of intense trial, but it is also a time of preparation. Just as God was with him in Potiphar's house, so too is God with Joseph in the prison. Once again, Joseph's character and faithfulness shine through. The prison warden recognizes that Joseph is a man of integrity and soon puts him in charge of the other prisoners. Even in the depths of the prison, God's favor is upon Joseph, and he continues to prosper, despite his circumstances.

It is during this time in prison that Joseph's gift for interpreting dreams comes into play once again. Two of Pharaoh's officials—the cupbearer and the baker—are thrown into prison with Joseph, and each of them has a troubling dream. Joseph, relying on the wisdom God has given him, interprets their dreams accurately. For the cupbearer, the dream foretells his restoration to Pharaoh's court, while for the baker, the dream predicts his execution.

Joseph's ability to interpret these dreams is not just a demonstration of his prophetic gift—it is a sign that God is still at work in his life. Even in the prison, God is preparing Joseph for the role he will one day play in saving Egypt and his family. But this preparation comes through suffering and waiting. Although Joseph asks the cupbearer to remember him when he is restored to his position, the cupbearer forgets Joseph, and he remains in prison for two more years.

This period of waiting is perhaps one of the most difficult aspects of Joseph's journey. He has been faithful, he has used his gifts to serve others, and yet he remains forgotten and imprisoned. But it is in this waiting that Joseph's character is refined. His story reminds us that God's timing is not our timing. Sometimes, the fulfillment of God's promises requires a season of waiting and endurance. Joseph's time in prison is a powerful reminder that even in the midst of trials, God is at work, preparing us for what lies ahead.

Pharaoh's Dreams And Joseph's Exaltation

After years of waiting, Joseph's moment of deliverance finally arrives. Pharaoh has two disturbing dreams that none of his advisors can interpret. It is then that the cupbearer remembers Joseph and tells Pharaoh about his ability to interpret dreams. Joseph is brought out of the prison and into Pharaoh's court, where he listens to Pharaoh's dreams.

Once again, Joseph relies on God for the interpretation. He tells Pharaoh that the dreams are a warning from God about seven years of abundance followed by seven years of severe famine. Joseph doesn't stop at interpreting the dreams—he offers Pharaoh a plan to prepare for the coming famine by storing up grain during the years of plenty. Pharaoh, recognizing that the Spirit of God is with Joseph, elevates him to the position of second-in-command over all of Egypt.

Joseph's rise to power is nothing short of miraculous. In an instant, he goes from being a prisoner to being the most powerful man in Egypt, second only to Pharaoh. This moment of exaltation is the fulfillment of the dreams Joseph had as a young man—dreams that his brothers had tried to destroy. But Joseph's rise to power is not just about his personal vindication. It is about God's plan to save many lives through him.

In this moment, we see the culmination of Joseph's journey from suffering to sovereignty. His years of betrayal, slavery, and imprisonment were not wasted. They were part of God's plan to prepare him for this moment. Joseph's story reminds us that God's purposes are often hidden in our suffering, but they are always working toward a greater good. Just as Joseph was exalted after years of suffering, so too are we called to trust that God is working all things together for our good, even when we cannot see the full picture.

A Prophetic Foreshadowing Of Christ

Joseph's journey from suffering to sovereignty is not just a personal story of redemption; it is a powerful prophetic foreshadowing of the life, death, and resurrection of Christ. Just as Joseph was betrayed by those closest to him, sold for pieces of silver, and cast into a pit, so too was Christ betrayed by His own disciple, sold for thirty pieces of silver, and sent to His death on a cross. But, like Joseph, Christ's suffering was not the end of the story—it was the path to His exaltation.

Joseph's rise from the pit to the palace mirrors Christ's resurrection and ascension. Joseph's suffering and endurance ultimately led to his being raised up as the savior of Egypt, providing food and sustenance during a time of famine. In the same way, Christ's death and resurrection opened the way for Him to provide spiritual sustenance to all who come to Him. Jesus is the ultimate fulfillment of the role that Joseph played in Egypt—He is the bread of life, the One who provides for our deepest spiritual hunger.

Additionally, Joseph's role in preserving his family—through whom the nation of Israel would be established—points forward to the greater role Christ plays in preserving and reconciling humanity. Just as Joseph's rise to power ensured the survival of his family during the famine, Christ's resurrection ensures the eternal life of all who trust in Him, saving us from the ultimate famine of separation from God.

Moreover, the revelation of Joseph's identity to his brothers, where they come to realize the one they betrayed is now their savior, is a profound foreshadowing of Christ's second coming. At His return, all of humanity will recognize Christ as Lord, including those who rejected Him. Just as Joseph's brothers feared for their lives when they realized who he was, so too will there be awe and reverence when Christ is revealed in His glory. Yet, like Joseph, Christ extends forgiveness and grace to those who seek reconciliation.

Theological Reflections On Suffering And Divine Sovereignty

Joseph's life teaches us a deep theological truth about suffering and God's sovereignty. Throughout his journey, Joseph experienced profound suffering—betrayal, slavery, and unjust imprisonment. Yet, at no point was God absent from his life. In fact, it was through these very trials that God was preparing Joseph for the greater purpose He had in mind.

This pattern of suffering leading to glory is a recurring theme throughout Scripture. In Romans 8:28, Paul writes, "And we know that in all things God works for the good of those who love Him, who have been called according to His purpose." Joseph's life exemplifies this truth. What his brothers intended for harm, God intended for good. This is a central theme not only in Joseph's story but in the entire biblical narrative—God is always at work, even in the darkest of circumstances, to bring about His redemptive purposes.

For believers, this truth offers a profound source of hope. Like Joseph, we may not always understand why we face certain trials, but we can trust that God is sovereign and that He is working behind the scenes. Our suffering is never wasted in the economy of God. Whether it's relational pain, career setbacks, or personal loss, God can use our suffering to shape us, refine our character, and ultimately bring about His purposes in our lives.

Moreover, Joseph's story reminds us that God's timing is perfect. Joseph endured many years of hardship before he saw the fulfillment of God's promises. His time in prison, though painful, was a period of preparation for the role he would eventually play in saving Egypt and his family. In the same way, we are often called to wait on God's timing. His delays are not denials—they are often periods of preparation, where God is working in us and through us to prepare us for the future He has in store.

Joseph's Faith As A Model For Endurance

Throughout his journey, Joseph demonstrates remarkable faith and endurance. In the face of betrayal, slavery, and injustice, Joseph never abandons his trust in God. Even when his circumstances seem bleak, he continues to serve faithfully and to trust that God has a plan for his life. Joseph's faith is not a passive resignation but an active trust in God's promises.

This kind of faith—one that endures through trials—is a model for us today. In the book of Hebrews, we are reminded that faith is the "assurance of things hoped for, the conviction of things not seen" (Hebrews 11:1). Joseph's life embodies this definition of faith. Though he could not see the full picture of God's plan, he trusted in what he could not see, holding fast to the promises God had given him in his dreams.

For believers, Joseph's faith challenges us to trust God even when our circumstances are difficult. It reminds us that faith is not just believing in God when things are going well—it is holding on to Him in the midst of trials, trusting that He is faithful and that He will fulfill His promises. Joseph's endurance through suffering is a powerful example of what it looks like to walk by faith and not by sight (2 Corinthians 5:7).

The Sovereignty Of God And The Fulfillment Of His Plan

Joseph's journey from suffering to sovereignty is not just a personal story of redemption—it is a testimony to the sovereign hand of God at work in history. Through every trial, every betrayal, and every moment of suffering, God was orchestrating a greater plan. What Joseph's brothers intended for evil, God intended for good. This is the mystery of divine providence—God is able to use even the sinful actions of humans to bring about His purposes.

Joseph's life is a reminder that God's plan is often hidden from us, but it is always unfolding according to His perfect timing. The years Joseph spent in slavery and in prison were not wasted—they were the crucible in which his character was forged and his faith was refined. In the same way, our own periods of suffering are often times of preparation for the greater purposes God has in store for us.

Ultimately, Joseph's story points us to the greater story of redemption that God is telling through Christ. Just as Joseph was betrayed, suffered, and was ultimately exalted, so too did Christ endure suffering and betrayal to bring about the salvation of the world. Joseph's journey from the pit to the palace is a shadow of the greater journey Christ took from the cross to the throne. And just as Joseph's suffering led to the preservation of his family, so too does Christ's suffering lead to the preservation and reconciliation of all who place their trust in Him.

Joseph's life is a powerful reminder that God is sovereign, that He is faithful, and that His purposes are always good. Even in our darkest moments, we can trust that God is at work, bringing about His redemptive plan in ways we cannot always see. And just as Joseph's story ended in glory, so too will our story end in the ultimate glory of Christ's return and the fulfillment of God's promises.

Chapter 9: Study Questions For Reflection

Joseph's Journey from Suffering to Sovereignty:

1. What does Joseph's journey teach us about enduring suffering and hardship?
2. How does Joseph's story illustrate God's providence and timing?
3. What role does forgiveness play in Joseph's life, and how can this be applied to our lives?
4. How does Joseph's role as a savior in Egypt foreshadow Christ's role as Savior?
5. What can we learn about preparation from Joseph's actions during the years of abundance?
6. In what ways did Joseph's suffering and subsequent exaltation foreshadow the suffering and resurrection of Christ?

CHAPTER 10: THE FEAST OF TRUMPETS—A CALL TO SPIRITUAL PREPARATION

The Feast of Trumpets, also known as Yom Teruah, is one of the most significant moments on the Jewish calendar. It marks the beginning of the High Holy Days and serves as a call to repentance, reflection, and spiritual readiness. Traditionally, the trumpet blast, or shofar, was a wake-up call to the people of Israel, signaling that the Day of Atonement was near and that it was time to prepare their hearts. The Feast of Trumpets reminds us of the importance of spiritual preparedness, not only for the immediate trials we may face but also for the ultimate day of reckoning and the return of the Messiah.

In Joseph's life, we see the practical outworking of this principle. His ability to interpret Pharaoh's dreams, which warned of a coming famine, was not just a display of his prophetic gift—it was a divine wake-up call. The years of abundance that Egypt was about to experience were a blessing, but Joseph's message made it clear that they were also a time for preparation. The Feast of Trumpets, with its call to spiritual readiness, parallels Joseph's call to Egypt and the surrounding nations to prepare for the famine that was coming.

The Role Of The Trumpet In Biblical History

Throughout Scripture, the trumpet is used as a symbol of divine intervention and a call to action. In the book of Exodus, the sound of the trumpet accompanied the giving of the Law at Mount Sinai (Exodus 19:16). It was a moment of awe and fear as the people gathered before the mountain to hear the voice of God. The trumpet blast announced the presence of God and called the people to attention.

In the book of Joshua, the trumpet played a central role in the fall of Jericho. God instructed the Israelites to march around the city for seven days, and on the seventh day, the priests were to blow the trumpets. When the people heard the sound, they were to shout, and the walls of the city would collapse (Joshua 6:20). Here again, the trumpet was a signal that God was about to act, and the people needed to be ready to follow His instructions.

The trumpet also appears in the prophetic writings, where it is often associated with the Day of the Lord. In Joel 2:1, we read, "Blow the trumpet in Zion; sound the alarm on my holy hill. Let all who live in the land tremble, for the day of the Lord is coming. It is close at hand." The trumpet blast in this context is a warning—a call to repentance and spiritual readiness as the day of judgment approaches.

In the New Testament, the trumpet continues to serve as a symbol of God's intervention in human history. Paul writes in 1 Corinthians 15:52 that the return of Christ will be accompanied by the sound of the trumpet: "In a flash, in the twinkling of an eye, at the last trumpet. For the trumpet will sound, the dead will be raised imperishable, and we will be changed." The trumpet, then, is not just a signal for the people of Israel—it is a signal for all of humanity that the time of reckoning is near.

Joseph's story fits within this larger biblical framework of the trumpet as a call to action. His interpretation of Pharaoh's dreams and his subsequent leadership in preparing for the famine serve as a metaphorical trumpet blast, calling Egypt to prepare for the difficult days ahead. The years of abundance were not meant to be wasted in complacency; they were a time of grace, a period in which the people could prepare for the coming hardship.

The Prophetic Significance Of Joseph's Leadership

Joseph's role in Egypt during the years of plenty and famine can be understood as a type of prophetic leadership. Much like the role of the prophets in Israel, Joseph was tasked with delivering a message of warning and calling the people to prepare. His leadership during this time was not just a matter of administrative skill—it was a reflection of his ability to discern God's plan and act in accordance with it.

The Feast of Trumpets, as a prophetic feast, is deeply connected to the theme of discernment. The trumpet blast is not just a call to action—it is a call to spiritual awareness. In Joseph's case, his ability to discern the meaning of Pharaoh's dreams allowed him to act wisely and prepare Egypt for the coming famine. He did not merely react to the crisis when it arrived; he saw it coming and made the necessary preparations well in advance.

This kind of spiritual discernment is at the heart of the Feast of Trumpets. The trumpet blast is a call to awaken from spiritual slumber and to be vigilant in recognizing the signs of the times. In our own lives, we are called to develop this same kind of discernment. Just as Joseph was able to see beyond the years of abundance to the famine that lay ahead, we are called to look beyond our present circumstances and recognize the spiritual realities that are often hidden beneath the surface.

The prophetic nature of Joseph's leadership also points us to the larger theme of God's sovereignty. Joseph's ability to interpret Pharaoh's dreams and his subsequent rise to power were not accidents—they were part of God's plan to preserve the people of Israel and fulfill His covenant promises. The Feast of Trumpets reminds us that God is always at work, even in the midst of difficult circumstances, and that His purposes will ultimately prevail.

Spiritual Readiness In Times Of Abundance

One of the key lessons from Joseph's story is the importance of spiritual readiness during times of abundance. It would have been easy for the people of Egypt to become complacent during the years of plenty. After all, the land was producing more than enough food, and there seemed to be no immediate threat on the horizon. But Joseph understood that these years of abundance were a gift from God—a time to prepare for the famine that was coming.

In the same way, the Feast of Trumpets calls us to recognize that times of spiritual abundance are not to be taken for granted. They are a gift from God, but they are also a time for preparation. Just as Joseph stored up grain during the years of plenty, we are called to store up spiritual resources during times of blessing. This means deepening our relationship with God, growing in our faith, and building up the spiritual disciplines that will sustain us during times of trial.

In our modern context, it is easy to become complacent in times of relative ease. When things are going well, we may be tempted to neglect our spiritual lives, assuming that the good times will last indefinitely. But Joseph's story reminds us that spiritual readiness is not just about reacting to crises—it is about preparing for them before they arrive. The Feast of Trumpets, with its call to wake up and prepare, serves as a reminder that we must always be vigilant, even in times of abundance.

Joseph's leadership during the years of plenty also teaches us about the importance of stewardship. He did not squander the resources that were available to him; instead, he managed them wisely, ensuring that there would be enough to sustain the people during the famine. In the same way, we are called to be good stewards of the spiritual resources God has given us. This means using our time, talents, and treasures in ways that honor God and prepare us for the challenges that may lie ahead.

The Trumpet Blast As A Call To Repentance

Another important aspect of the Feast of Trumpets is its connection to repentance. The trumpet blast is not just a call to action—it is a call to examine our hearts and turn back to God. In the context of Joseph's story, this theme of repentance can be seen in the way his brothers are eventually reconciled to him.

When the famine strikes, Joseph's brothers come to Egypt seeking food, unaware that the man they are dealing with is their long-lost brother. Joseph recognizes them, but they do not recognize him. Over the course of several encounters, Joseph tests his brothers to see if they have truly repented for what they did to him years earlier. These tests ultimately lead to a moment of reconciliation, where Joseph reveals his identity and forgives his brothers for their betrayal.

This moment of reconciliation is a powerful example of the kind of repentance and forgiveness that the Feast of Trumpets calls us to. Just as Joseph's brothers had to confront their past sins and seek forgiveness, we too are called to examine our hearts and turn back to God. The trumpet blast serves as a reminder that the time for repentance is now. We cannot wait until the famine arrives to get our spiritual house in order—we must be ready before the crisis comes.

The Feast of Trumpets also points us to the ultimate day of judgment, when Christ will return and the final trumpet will sound. In that moment, there will be no more time for repentance—our fate will be sealed. Joseph's story serves as a warning that we must not delay in turning back to God. The time for repentance is now, and the trumpet blast is a wake-up call to prepare our hearts for the coming of the Lord.

The Eschatological Significance Of The Trumpet Blast

The trumpet is not only a symbol of spiritual readiness in the present—it also points us forward to the future. In the New Testament, the trumpet blast is associated with the return of Christ and the final judgment. Paul writes in 1 Thessalonians 4:16-17, "For the Lord himself will come down from heaven, with a loud command, with the voice of the archangel and with the trumpet call of God, and the dead in Christ will rise first. After that, we who are still alive and are "left will be caught up together with them in the clouds to meet the Lord in the air. And so we will be with the Lord forever." The trumpet blast at Christ's return will signal the end of history as we know it and the beginning of God's final judgment and restoration of all things.

In Joseph's story, we see a precursor to this eschatological reality. Just as Joseph's leadership during the famine preserved life and ensured the survival of his family, so too will Christ's return bring salvation to His people and judgment to the world. The Feast of Trumpets is a reminder that we are living in the "in-between" time—between Christ's first coming and His return—and that we must remain spiritually ready, prepared for the final trumpet blast that will signal the end of this age.

The eschatological significance of the trumpet blast should

not be underestimated. It is a wake-up call to the church and to the world, reminding us that history is moving toward a definitive conclusion. The Feast of Trumpets, celebrated annually by the people of Israel, was a rehearsal for the final trumpet blast that will mark the culmination of God's redemptive plan. In the same way, Joseph's preparation for the famine was not just a reaction to a temporary crisis—it was part of God's larger plan to preserve the family through whom the Messiah would come.

For believers, the sound of the trumpet is a symbol of hope and anticipation. It is a reminder that Christ will return, that death will be defeated, and that we will be united with Him forever. But it is also a call to action, a call to live with urgency and purpose, knowing that our time on this earth is limited and that the final judgment is coming. Joseph's ability to discern the future and act accordingly is a model for us as we live in anticipation of Christ's return. We are called to be vigilant, to prepare our hearts, and to live in light of the coming kingdom.

Joseph's Example Of Vigilance And Faithfulness

One of the most striking aspects of Joseph's life is his unwavering vigilance and faithfulness to God's calling, even in the midst of hardship. From his betrayal by his brothers to his unjust imprisonment, Joseph never lost sight of God's promises or his duty to remain faithful in whatever circumstances he found himself. In times of plenty and in times of famine, Joseph was alert to God's leading and faithful in his service.

Joseph's faithfulness during the years of abundance is particularly noteworthy. It would have been easy for him to become complacent, enjoying the prosperity of Egypt and assuming that the good times would last indefinitely. But Joseph understood that the years of plenty were not an end in themselves—they were a time to prepare for what was coming. His vigilance during this time ensured that Egypt and the surrounding nations would survive the famine.

In the same way, the Feast of Trumpets calls us to be spiritually vigilant. It is easy to become complacent in times of blessing, to assume that our spiritual prosperity will continue without interruption. But Joseph's example reminds us that times of blessing are often a period of preparation for future trials. The trumpet blast is a reminder that we must always be ready, storing up spiritual resources, deepening our faith, and strengthening our relationship with God so that we can endure whatever may come.

Joseph's faithfulness also points us to the importance of trusting in God's timing. The years of abundance were followed by years of famine, but Joseph did not waver in his trust that God's plan would be fulfilled. His ability to discern the signs of the times and act accordingly is a model for us as we navigate the challenges of our own lives. The Feast of Trumpets reminds us that we live in a time of preparation, and we must remain faithful, even when we do not fully understand what God is doing.

Spiritual Preparation For The Return Of The King

Ultimately, the Feast of Trumpets points us forward to the return of Christ, the King of kings. Just as the trumpet blast in Joseph's story signaled the need for physical preparation for the famine, the trumpet blast at Christ's return will signal the need for spiritual preparation. Jesus Himself warns us to be ready for His coming, saying in Matthew 24:42, "Therefore keep watch, because you do not know on what day your Lord will come."

Joseph's life serves as a powerful reminder of the importance of this spiritual readiness. He did not wait until the famine arrived to begin preparing—he acted in advance, storing up grain during the years of plenty so that there would be enough to sustain the people during the years of hardship. In the same way, we are called to prepare for the return of Christ by storing up spiritual treasures, growing in our faith, and living in obedience to His Word.

The trumpet blast is a call to spiritual urgency. It reminds us that we are not promised tomorrow, and that the time to prepare is now. Joseph's leadership during the years of abundance serves as a metaphor for our own spiritual lives. Just as Joseph did not waste the years of plenty, we are called not to waste the time we have been given. Every moment is an opportunity to grow in our relationship with God, to serve others, and to prepare for the day when Christ will return.

The Feast of Trumpets, then, is not just a historical observance or a prophetic symbol—it is a call to action. It is a reminder that we must live with the end in mind, recognizing that our time on this earth is limited and that Christ will one day return to establish His kingdom. Joseph's life teaches us that spiritual preparation is not just about surviving the trials of this life—it is about being ready for the ultimate fulfillment of God's promises.

The Trumpet Call To Wakefulness And Faithfulness

As we reflect on the Feast of Trumpets and its connection to Joseph's story, we are reminded of the importance of spiritual wakefulness and faithfulness. The trumpet blast is a call to attention—a divine wake-up call that reminds us of the urgency of the moment. In Joseph's life, the years of abundance were not a time for complacency—they were a time for preparation. In the same way, the trumpet blast in our own lives calls us to prepare our hearts for the return of Christ and the coming kingdom.

Joseph's ability to discern the signs of the times and act accordingly is a model for us as we seek to live in spiritual readiness. The Feast of Trumpets calls us to be vigilant, to repent, and to prepare for the day when the final trumpet will sound. And just as Joseph's leadership preserved life during the famine, so too will our spiritual preparedness preserve us in the trials to come.

The trumpet blast is not just a call to action—it is a call to hope. It reminds us that Christ will return, that His kingdom will be established, and that we will one day be united with Him in glory. But until that day comes, we are called to live with urgency, preparing our hearts and our lives for the return of the King. Joseph's story reminds us that God is always at work, even in the midst of uncertainty, and that His plans will ultimately be fulfilled. As we await the final trumpet, may we be found faithful, ready to meet our Lord when He comes.

Chapter 10: Study Questions For Reflection

Joseph: A Type of the 6th Seal and the Feasts:

1. How does Joseph's decision to forgive his brothers reflect the spirit of the Feast of Atonement, which focuses on repentance and reconciliation with God?

2. In what ways does Joseph test his brothers' hearts before fully reconciling with them? What does this teach us about the process of genuine reconciliation?

3. Reflect on a time when you were in need of forgiveness or when you extended forgiveness to someone else. How did the process of reconciliation impact you or the other person involved?

4. What role does humility play in both giving and receiving forgiveness, as seen in the interactions between Joseph and his brothers?

5. How can we apply Joseph's example of grace and forgiveness to relationships in our own lives, particularly in situations where we have been deeply hurt or betrayed?

6. The Feast of Atonement is about restoring relationships with God and with others. How can you seek to reconcile broken relationships in your life and draw closer to God in the process?

CHAPTER 11: PROVISION IN THE FAMINE—JOSEPH AS A PROPHETIC PROVIDER

Joseph's rise to power in Egypt is one of the most dramatic reversals of fortune in all of Scripture. From the depths of slavery and imprisonment, Joseph ascends to become the second most powerful man in Egypt, entrusted with the responsibility of managing the nation's resources during a time of both abundance and crisis. This aspect of Joseph's life—his role as a provider during the famine—serves not only as a remarkable example of leadership and stewardship but also as a profound prophetic foreshadowing of Christ's role as the ultimate provider.

The seven years of abundance that preceded the famine were a time of immense prosperity for Egypt. The land produced bountifully, and under Joseph's leadership, the grain was stored in vast quantities to prepare for the years of scarcity that were to follow. Joseph's wisdom and foresight, gifts from God, enabled him to prepare Egypt and the surrounding nations for the impending famine. In this way, Joseph becomes a figure who reflects the divine provision that would ultimately be fulfilled in Christ, who provides not only for our physical needs but also for our spiritual hunger.

Joseph's Role As A Provider: A Reflection Of Divine Wisdom

The story of Joseph's provision during the famine highlights a key theme that runs throughout Scripture: the idea that God provides for His people, even in times of great need. Joseph's ability to interpret Pharaoh's dreams and to implement a plan for managing the resources of Egypt was not simply a display of human ingenuity. It was a manifestation of divine wisdom, a gift from God that allowed Joseph to discern the times and to act in accordance with God's plan.

In Genesis 41:25, Joseph says to Pharaoh, "The dreams of Pharaoh are one and the same. God has revealed to Pharaoh what he is about to do." From the outset, Joseph makes it clear that the wisdom he possesses is not his own—it is a revelation from God. This understanding is central to Joseph's success as a provider during the famine. His ability to see beyond the present moment and to prepare for the future was a gift from God, and it was this divine insight that enabled him to save many lives.

Joseph's role as a provider is a reflection of the way God provides for His people throughout history. In the wilderness, God provided manna from heaven to sustain the Israelites during their journey to the Promised Land. In the same way, God provided for Elijah during the drought, sending ravens to bring him food by the brook Cherith (1 Kings 17:2-6). These stories of divine provision are not merely about physical sustenance—they point to the deeper reality that God is the ultimate source of all that we need, both physically and spiritually.

Joseph's leadership during the years of famine also reflects the importance of stewardship. He did not waste the resources that were entrusted to him; instead, he managed them wisely, ensuring that there would be enough to sustain the people during the years of scarcity. In this way, Joseph's actions serve as a model for us as we seek to be good stewards of the resources God has given us. Whether in times of abundance or in times of want, we are called to manage what we have been given in a way that honors God and provides for the needs of others.

The Prophetic Significance Of Joseph's Provision

While Joseph's role as a provider during the famine was undoubtedly a matter of practical leadership, it also carries deep prophetic significance. In many ways, Joseph's provision for Egypt and the surrounding nations serves as a foreshadowing of the provision that Christ would ultimately offer to the world.

Just as Joseph provided grain to sustain life during the famine, Christ offers Himself as the "bread of life," providing spiritual sustenance to all who come to Him. In John 6:35, Jesus declares, "I am the bread of life. Whoever comes to me will never go hungry, and whoever believes in me will never be thirsty." This statement points to the deeper reality that, just as physical food sustains the body, Christ's presence and His sacrificial work sustain our souls.

The famine in Joseph's time was a physical manifestation of a deeper spiritual famine that humanity experiences apart from God. Without the provision of food, the people of Egypt and the surrounding nations would have perished. In the same way, without the provision of Christ's sacrifice, humanity would be lost in spiritual starvation. Joseph's provision of grain during the famine becomes a prophetic picture of Christ's provision for our spiritual hunger—a hunger that can only be satisfied by the One who offers Himself as the true bread from heaven.

Furthermore, the fact that Joseph's provision extended beyond the borders of Egypt to the surrounding nations highlights the universal scope of God's provision through Christ. Joseph did not hoard the grain for Egypt alone; he opened the storehouses to all who came seeking food. This inclusiveness points to the way in which Christ's sacrifice is offered to all people, regardless of nationality, race, or background. Just as Joseph's provision saved lives during the famine, Christ's sacrifice offers eternal life to all who believe in Him.

The Famine As A Metaphor For Spiritual Need

The seven years of famine in Egypt serve as a powerful metaphor for the spiritual famine that exists in the world. Just as the physical famine left the people of Egypt and the surrounding nations desperate for food, so too does spiritual famine leave humanity longing for meaning, purpose, and connection with God. The absence of physical nourishment in the land mirrors the absence of spiritual nourishment in the hearts of those who are separated from God.

In Amos 8:11, the prophet speaks of a different kind of famine, one that is not about the absence of bread or water but the absence of God's Word: "The days are coming, declares the Sovereign Lord, when I will send a famine through the land—not a famine of food or a thirst for water, but a famine of hearing the words of the Lord." This spiritual famine is even more devastating than the physical famine that Joseph managed, for it affects the soul rather than the body.

Joseph's role as a provider during the famine becomes a prophetic picture of the way Christ provides for us in the midst of our spiritual hunger. Without the Word of God, without the bread of life, we are left starving, searching for meaning in a world that cannot satisfy our deepest longings. But just as Joseph opened the storehouses of Egypt to feed the hungry, Christ opens His arms to all who come to Him, offering them the sustenance they need to live abundantly in this life and in the life to come.

The famine in Egypt also serves as a reminder that periods of spiritual dryness are not uncommon in the Christian life. There are times when we may feel distant from God, when our souls seem parched, and when we struggle to find spiritual nourishment. In these times, we are called to turn to Christ, who offers Himself as the source of living water (John 4:14). Joseph's provision during the famine reminds us that God is faithful to provide for us, even in seasons of spiritual drought. He invites us to come to Him and be filled, to draw near to Him and find the sustenance our souls crave.

Joseph's Provision And The Role Of The Church

Joseph's role as a provider during the famine also points to the role of the Church as a provider of both physical and spiritual nourishment in the world. Just as Joseph was entrusted with the resources of Egypt and called to distribute them wisely, the Church has been entrusted with the gospel—the good news of Christ's saving work—and called to share it with the world.

In Matthew 28:19, Jesus commissions His disciples to "go and make disciples of all nations." This Great Commission is a call for the Church to act as a provider, offering the bread of life to a world that is starving for truth and meaning. The Church, like Joseph, is called to open its storehouses and provide for the spiritual needs of all who come seeking. This means not only preaching the gospel but also living it out through acts of service, love, and compassion.

The Church is also called to be a place of refuge in times of crisis, much like Egypt was during the famine. When the world is in turmoil, when people are searching for hope and stability, the Church is called to be a place of provision—a place where people can come to find the nourishment they need, both physically and spiritually. Just as Joseph's leadership provided a way for Egypt and the surrounding nations to survive the famine, the Church is called to provide a way for people to experience the life-giving grace of Christ.

Furthermore, Joseph's example reminds the Church of the importance of stewardship. Just as Joseph was entrusted with the resources of Egypt and called to manage them wisely, the Church has been entrusted with the gospel and called to steward it faithfully. This means sharing the good news with others, but it also means using our resources—our time, talents, and treasures—in ways that honor God and advance His kingdom. Joseph's leadership during the famine is a model for how the Church can use its resources to meet both the physical and spiritual needs of the world.

The Feast Of Trumpets And The Call To Provision

As we reflect on Joseph's role as a provider during the famine, we can see how his story ties into the themes of the Feast of Trumpets. The trumpet blast is a call to prepare—not just for physical trials but for spiritual ones as well. Joseph's preparation during the years of abundance was a response to the divine warning given through Pharaoh's dreams, and it ensured that there would be enough provision to sustain the people during the famine.

In the same way, the Feast of Trumpets calls us to prepare for spiritual challenges, reminding us that times of abundance are not simply times to enjoy prosperity but are also times to store up spiritual resources for the trials that may come. Just as Joseph did not wait until the famine arrived to begin preparing, we are called to use the times of spiritual abundance to deepen our faith, grow in our relationship with God, and strengthen our spiritual disciplines.

Joseph's provision during the famine can be seen as a prophetic foreshadowing of the Church's role in the last days. Just as Joseph was entrusted with the physical resources to sustain life during the famine, the Church is entrusted with the spiritual resources needed to sustain life in the face of spiritual famine. The trumpet blast of the Feast of Trumpets is a call to awaken the Church to this responsibility. It is a reminder that we are living in a time of preparation, a time when we must be vigilant in providing for the spiritual needs of those around us.

The Feast of Trumpets also serves as a reminder that God's provision is not limited to the physical realm. Just as Joseph provided for the physical needs of Egypt and the surrounding nations, God provides for our spiritual needs in Christ. The trumpet blast is a call to recognize that our true sustenance comes not from the things of this world but from the bread of life that Christ offers. In John 6:27, Jesus says, "Do not work for food that spoils, but for food that endures to eternal life, which the Son of Man will give you." This is the spiritual provision that Joseph's story points to—a provision that goes beyond the temporary relief of physical hunger and addresses the eternal hunger of the soul.

Joseph's Leadership As A Model Of Christ's Provision

As we continue to reflect on Joseph's role as a provider, it becomes clear that his leadership during the famine serves as a model of Christ's provision for us. Just as Joseph provided for the physical needs of Egypt, Christ provides for our spiritual needs in ways that are far more profound and eternal. Joseph's leadership was marked by wisdom, foresight, and compassion—all qualities that are perfectly embodied in Christ.

First, Joseph's wisdom in preparing for the famine mirrors Christ's wisdom in guiding us through the trials of life. In the same way that Joseph discerned the future and acted accordingly, Christ knows the challenges we will face and prepares us for them. His teachings, His example, and His promises provide us with the spiritual resources we need to navigate the storms of life. In Matthew 7:24-27, Jesus compares those who hear His words and put them into practice to a wise man who builds his house on the rock. When the storms come, the house stands firm because it is built on a solid foundation. Joseph's wisdom in preparing for the famine points us to the wisdom of Christ, who teaches us how to build our lives on the solid foundation of His Word.

Second, Joseph's foresight in storing up grain during the years of abundance reflects Christ's foresight in providing for our spiritual needs before we even realize them. Just as Joseph anticipated the famine and acted in advance to ensure that there would be enough food, Christ provided for our salvation long before we understood our need for it. In Romans 5:8, Paul writes, "But God demonstrates his own love for us in this: While we were still sinners, Christ died for us." Christ's provision for our spiritual hunger was made long before we realized how desperately we needed it, just as Joseph's provision was made before the famine struck.

Finally, Joseph's compassion for those who came to him for food mirrors Christ's compassion for those who come to Him seeking spiritual nourishment. In the same way that Joseph opened the storehouses of Egypt to all who were in need, Christ opens His arms to all who come to Him in faith. In Matthew 11:28, Jesus says, "Come to me, all you who are weary and burdened, and I will give you rest." Joseph's compassionate provision during the famine is a reflection of Christ's compassion for us, a compassion that meets us in our need and provides for us abundantly.

The Spiritual And Prophetic Dimensions Of Provision

The story of Joseph's provision during the famine is not just a historical account of a wise leader managing resources—it is a prophetic picture of the way God provides for His people, both physically and spiritually. Just as Joseph's provision sustained life during the famine, God's provision sustains us in times of spiritual famine. This provision is not only for our physical needs but also for our deepest spiritual longings.

Throughout Scripture, we see the theme of provision woven into the fabric of God's relationship with His people. In the wilderness, God provided manna from heaven to sustain the Israelites during their journey. In the ministry of Jesus, we see the miraculous feeding of the five thousand, where Jesus takes five loaves of bread and two fish and multiplies them to feed the crowd (Matthew 14:13-21). These acts of provision point to the ultimate provision that God offers in Christ, who gives His body and blood as the true bread of life (John 6:51).

Joseph's story also points to the eschatological dimension of provision. The famine that Joseph prepared for can be seen as a metaphor for the spiritual famine that will come in the last days —a time when people will hunger and thirst for truth, but it will be in short supply. In this context, Joseph's provision during the famine serves as a prophetic picture of the way Christ will provide for His people during the final days of human history. Just as Joseph's leadership ensured the survival of Egypt and the surrounding nations, Christ's leadership will ensure the survival of His people during the trials of the end times.

In the book of Revelation, we see a similar theme of provision in the new heavens and the new earth, where God will provide for His people in ways that go beyond anything we can imagine. Revelation 7:16-17 says, "Never again will they hunger; never again will they thirst. The sun will not beat down on them, nor any scorching heat. For the Lamb at the center of the throne will be their shepherd; 'he will lead them to springs of living water.'" This ultimate provision is the fulfillment of what Joseph's story points to—the eternal provision of Christ, who meets all of our needs, both now and in the age to come.

The Prophetic Provider And The Call To Trust In God's Provision

As we conclude our reflection on Joseph's role as a prophetic provider, we are reminded that his story is not just about a wise leader managing resources during a time of crisis—it is a story that points us to the ultimate provider, Christ, who meets both our physical and spiritual needs. Just as Joseph's provision sustained life during the famine, Christ's provision sustains us in the midst of our spiritual hunger and thirst.

Joseph's leadership during the years of abundance and famine serves as a model for us as we seek to live in trust and reliance on God's provision. Whether we are in a season of abundance or a season of famine, we can trust that God is faithful to provide for us, just as He provided for Joseph and the people of Egypt. The trumpet blast of the Feast of Trumpets calls us to prepare, to store up spiritual resources, and to trust in the provision that God offers through Christ.

In the same way that Joseph opened the storehouses of Egypt to all who were in need, Christ opens His arms to all who come to Him, offering the bread of life that sustains us now and forever. As we live in anticipation of the final trumpet blast—the return of Christ—we are called to trust in His provision, knowing that He is faithful to provide for all of our needs, both in this life and in the life to come.

Chapter 11: Study Questions For Reflection

Restoration of the Family—The Spiritual Temple:

1. How does Joseph's restoration of his family reflect God's desire to restore broken relationships with His people?
2. What role does forgiveness and grace play in the healing of Joseph's family? How can you apply these principles to relationships in your life?
3. In what ways have you experienced restoration in your life after a season of trial?

CHAPTER 12: THE UNVEILING OF GOD'S PLAN

*From Hidden to Revealed and
The Feast of Atonement—
Forgiveness and Reconciliation*

The story of Joseph is one that reveals the often hidden hand of God at work in human history. From the time of his dreams as a young boy to his eventual rise to power in Egypt, Joseph's life demonstrates how God's purposes, though often concealed, are always unfolding toward a greater good. Joseph's journey is a testament to the mystery of divine providence—a reminder that while we may not always understand the circumstances we face, we can trust that God is always at work, orchestrating events for His glory and our ultimate good.

The unveiling of God's plan in Joseph's life did not happen all at once. It was a process that unfolded gradually, often through trials and suffering. Yet, through each step of his journey, Joseph remained faithful, trusting that the God who had given him the dreams would also bring them to fulfillment. This chapter will explore the ways in which God's plan was revealed in Joseph's life, and how his story serves as a model for us as we seek to understand the often hidden purposes of God in our own lives.

The Early Dreams: A Glimpse Of God's Plan

Joseph's story begins with a series of dreams that, at the time, must have seemed both mysterious and perplexing. In Genesis 37, Joseph dreams that he and his brothers are binding sheaves of grain in the field, and suddenly, his sheaf rises and stands upright while his brothers' sheaves gather around it and bow down to it (Genesis 37:7). In a second dream, Joseph sees the sun, moon, and eleven stars bowing down to him (Genesis 37:9).

These dreams are a prophetic glimpse of what is to come —an early revelation of the plan that God has for Joseph's life. Yet, at the time, neither Joseph nor his family fully understood their significance. In fact, the dreams only served to deepen the tension between Joseph and his brothers, who were already jealous of their father's favoritism toward him. Joseph's brothers interpreted the dreams as a sign of arrogance, and their resentment grew to the point where they plotted to rid themselves of him altogether.

At this early stage in Joseph's life, the dreams seem almost out of place. How could a young boy, the second youngest of twelve brothers, ever imagine that his siblings and even his parents would bow down to him? And yet, these dreams were a glimpse into the future—a future that only God could see. The dreams were not meant to inflate Joseph's ego; they were a prophetic foretelling of the role that Joseph would one day play in the preservation of his family.

In many ways, the early dreams in Joseph's life serve as a reminder of how God often gives us glimpses of His plan without revealing the full picture. There are moments in our lives when we sense that God is leading us in a certain direction, but the path ahead is still unclear. Like Joseph, we may have a sense of the destination, but we do not yet know the journey that will take us there. These early glimpses of God's plan can be both exciting and perplexing, as we wonder how the pieces of our lives will fit together. Yet, Joseph's story reminds us that even when we cannot see the full picture, God's plan is always unfolding according to His perfect timing.

Betrayal And The Pit: The Hidden Hand Of God In Suffering

After Joseph's dreams, the trajectory of his life takes a dramatic turn. His brothers, fueled by jealousy and resentment, conspire to throw him into a pit and sell him into slavery. What must have seemed like the death of Joseph's dreams was, in reality, the beginning of God's plan to bring them to fulfillment.

Joseph's time in the pit and his subsequent sale into slavery in Egypt serve as a powerful reminder that God's plan is often hidden in the midst of suffering. In the moment, Joseph could not have known that his betrayal by his brothers would be the catalyst for his rise to power in Egypt. All he could see was the immediate pain of being abandoned by his family and sold into slavery. Yet, even in the darkest moments of Joseph's life, God's hand was at work, guiding him toward the future that He had prepared.

The pit, in many ways, is a metaphor for the times in our lives when we feel abandoned, lost, and without hope. Like Joseph, we may find ourselves in situations where it seems as though God's plan for our lives has been derailed. Yet, Joseph's story teaches us that even in the pit, God is present. His plan is never thwarted by human actions, and what may seem like a detour or a dead end is often the very means by which God brings His purposes to pass.

This theme of hiddenness is central to the story of Joseph and, indeed, to much of the biblical narrative. God often works behind the scenes, using what appear to be setbacks or failures to accomplish His greater purposes. In the case of Joseph, the very act of betrayal that seemed to signal the end of his dreams was, in fact, the beginning of their fulfillment. God was using the actions of Joseph's brothers to set in motion a plan that would not only save Joseph but also preserve the entire nation of Israel.

From Slave To Prisoner: The Long Road To Fulfillment

Joseph's journey from the pit to the palace was not an overnight success story. After being sold into slavery in Egypt, Joseph was purchased by Potiphar, a high-ranking official in Pharaoh's court. For a time, it seemed as though Joseph's fortunes were improving. He found favor in Potiphar's eyes and was put in charge of his entire household. Yet, even in this position of relative stability, Joseph's path took another unexpected turn when Potiphar's wife falsely accused him of attempted assault, leading to his imprisonment.

Once again, Joseph found himself in a situation that seemed far removed from the dreams of his youth. He had gone from being a favored son to a slave and now to a prisoner. But even in the prison, God's plan was at work. In Genesis 39:21, we read that "the Lord was with Joseph and showed him steadfast love and gave him favor in the sight of the keeper of the prison." Despite the injustice of his circumstances, Joseph continued to trust in God's faithfulness.

Joseph's time in prison serves as a reminder that God's plan often involves seasons of waiting and testing. The road to fulfillment is not always straightforward, and there are times when we may feel as though we are stuck in a place of limitation or confinement. Yet, Joseph's story teaches us that even in these seasons of waiting, God is at work. The prison was not the end of Joseph's story—it was a place of preparation for the role that God had for him in the future.

It is in the prison that Joseph's gift of interpreting dreams once again comes to the forefront. When two of Pharaoh's officials, the cupbearer and the baker, are thrown into prison with Joseph, they each have a dream that they cannot interpret. Joseph, relying on the wisdom and insight that God had given him, interprets their dreams with accuracy. For the cupbearer, the dream foretold his restoration to Pharaoh's service, while for the baker, the dream predicted his execution.

Joseph's ability to interpret these dreams was not just a demonstration of his prophetic gift—it was a sign that God's hand was still upon him, even in the prison. Joseph's gift of interpretation would eventually lead to his release from prison and his rise to power in Egypt, but for the time being, he remained in the prison, waiting for God's plan to be fully revealed.

The Unveiling In Pharaoh's Court: God's Timing And Providence

After two years of waiting, Joseph's moment of deliverance finally arrived. Pharaoh, the ruler of Egypt, had two troubling dreams that none of his advisors could interpret. It was then that the cupbearer, who had been restored to his position in Pharaoh's court, remembered Joseph and told Pharaoh about his ability to interpret dreams. Joseph was brought out of the prison and into Pharaoh's court, where he interpreted the dreams as a warning from God about seven years of abundance followed by seven years of severe famine.

Joseph's interpretation of Pharaoh's dreams was not only accurate but also accompanied by a plan of action. He advised Pharaoh to appoint a wise and discerning man to oversee the collection and storage of grain during the years of abundance, so that there would be enough to sustain the nation during the years of famine. Pharaoh, recognizing the wisdom of Joseph's counsel, appointed him as the second-in-command over all of Egypt.

This moment of unveiling in Pharaoh's court was the culmination of years of waiting, suffering, and preparation. The dreams that Joseph had as a young boy were finally coming to pass, though not in the way he had initially imagined. His brothers, who had sold him into slavery, would one day come to Egypt seeking food, and they would bow down before him, just as his dreams had foretold.

Yet, the fulfillment of Joseph's dreams was not about personal vindication or revenge. Joseph understood that his rise to power was not for his own glory but for the preservation of life. In Genesis 45:7, Joseph says to his brothers, "God sent me before you to preserve for you a remnant on earth, and to keep alive for you many survivors." Joseph's story is a powerful reminder that the fulfillment of God's plan in our lives is always for a greater purpose—one that often goes beyond our personal desires or ambitions.

The Theological Significance Of Hiddenness And Revelation

Joseph's life provides a profound theological reflection on the nature of God's hiddenness and revelation. Throughout Scripture, we see that God often works behind the scenes, in ways that are hidden from human understanding. Yet, in His perfect timing, God reveals His plan, bringing to light what was once concealed.

This theme of hiddenness and revelation is central to the biblical narrative. In Deuteronomy 29:29, we read, "The secret things belong to the Lord our God, but the things revealed belong to us and to our children forever, that we may follow all the words of this law." There are aspects of God's plan that remain hidden from us, and we may never fully understand them in this life. Yet, God is always at work, revealing His purposes in His own time and in His own way.

In Joseph's life, we see the unfolding of God's plan over the course of many years. From the early dreams to the betrayal by his brothers, from slavery to imprisonment, and finally to his rise to power in Egypt, Joseph's story is a testament to the slow and often painful process of revelation. But through it all, Joseph remained faithful, trusting that the God who had given him the dreams would also bring them to fulfillment.

For us, Joseph's story serves as an encouragement to trust in God's timing, even when His plan seems hidden from view. There are times in our lives when we may feel as though we are in the pit or the prison, far from the fulfillment of the dreams and promises God has given us. Yet, Joseph's story reminds us that God is always at work, and that His plan, though often hidden, is always moving toward revelation and fulfillment.

Living In The Tension Of Hiddenness And Revelation

As we reflect on the unveiling of God's plan in Joseph's life, we are reminded that we, too, live in the tension between hiddenness and revelation. There are aspects of God's plan that remain hidden from us, and we may not always understand the circumstances we face. Yet, Joseph's story encourages us to trust in the faithfulness of God, knowing that His purposes are always unfolding, even when we cannot see them.

The unveiling of God's plan in Joseph's life teaches us that waiting, suffering, and uncertainty are often part of the process of revelation. Like Joseph, we are called to remain faithful in the midst of trials, trusting that God's hand is at work, even when His plan seems hidden. And when the time is right, God will reveal His purposes, bringing to light what was once concealed and fulfilling His promises in ways that go beyond our understanding.

In Joseph's story, we see the mystery of divine providence at work—a reminder that God's plan is always moving from hiddenness to revelation, from darkness to light. As we live in the tension of the "already" and the "not yet," may we find comfort in the knowledge that God is faithful, and that His plan, though hidden, is always unfolding toward a greater good.

As God's plan moves from hidden to revealed, we see not only His sovereignty but also His heart for reconciliation—a theme central to the Feast of Atonement. Just as Joseph's life unveils God's redemptive purpose, the path to forgiveness and restored relationships further reveals His desire for unity and grace. Through this journey, Joseph's story becomes not only a narrative of endurance and divine orchestration but also a powerful reflection of the Atonement's call to repentance and reconciliation.

The Feast of Atonement—
Forgiveness and Reconciliation

The story of Joseph and his brothers is a remarkable narrative of broken relationships, deep betrayal, and eventual reconciliation. It is a story that mirrors the core themes of the Feast of Atonement—a sacred day in the Jewish calendar dedicated to repentance, forgiveness, and the restoration of relationships with both God and others. As we explore Joseph's journey toward forgiveness and reconciliation with his brothers, we will see how his story serves as a prophetic picture of the ultimate atonement that would come through Christ, offering a pathway for us to reflect on the profound work of forgiveness in our own lives.

The Feast of Atonement, or *Yom Kippur*, is a time for deep introspection, repentance, and reconciliation. It is a day when the people of Israel would humble themselves before God, seeking forgiveness for their sins and making amends for any wrongs they had committed against others. At the heart of this sacred day is the understanding that forgiveness is not only about individual restoration but also about the healing of relationships and the reestablishment of communal harmony. In the story of Joseph, we see these themes play out on a personal level as Joseph confronts his brothers, tests their hearts, and ultimately extends forgiveness, offering a path to reconciliation that reflects the heart of the Feast of Atonement.

The Context Of Betrayal: A Family Torn Apart

Before we can fully understand the significance of forgiveness and reconciliation in Joseph's story, we must first revisit the context of the betrayal that tore his family apart. Joseph's brothers, consumed by jealousy and resentment, conspired to rid themselves of him by selling him into slavery. This act of betrayal was not just a familial conflict—it was a deeply personal violation that left Joseph isolated from his family and thrust into a life of servitude in a foreign land.

For Joseph's brothers, the act of selling him into slavery may have seemed like a way to eliminate the source of their envy, but it created a wound that would fester for years. The brothers carried the guilt of their actions, even as they tried to suppress it. In Genesis 42:21, after Joseph begins to test them, they express their remorse: "Surely we are being punished because of our brother. We saw how distressed he was when he pleaded with us for his life, but we would not listen; that's why this distress has come on us." Their words reveal that, though years had passed, the weight of their sin had never left them.

The brothers' betrayal created a fracture in the family that could only be healed through a process of repentance and forgiveness. Their relationship with Joseph was not the only one damaged by their actions—their relationship with their father, Jacob, was also strained by the deception they used to cover up their crime. The Feast of Atonement speaks to this kind of brokenness, reminding us that sin not only separates us from God but also from one another. It creates a web of relational dysfunction that can only be untangled through the work of repentance, forgiveness, and reconciliation.

The Testing Of The Brothers: A Path To Repentance

When Joseph's brothers first come to Egypt seeking food during the famine, they do not recognize him. Joseph, however, recognizes them immediately. This moment presents Joseph with a choice: he could reveal himself and seek revenge for the betrayal, or he could begin the process of reconciliation. Joseph chooses the latter, but not before testing his brothers to see if they have truly repented for their past actions.

Joseph's tests are not acts of cruelty; rather, they are designed to reveal whether his brothers have changed. In Genesis 42:7-17, Joseph accuses them of being spies and places them in custody for three days. After this, he releases them but demands that they bring their youngest brother, Benjamin, to Egypt as proof of their honesty. This demand is significant because Benjamin, as the youngest son and the only remaining child of Rachel, is now Jacob's favored son, much like Joseph had once been. The brothers' willingness to risk bringing Benjamin to Egypt would demonstrate whether they had learned from their past mistake of betraying a favored sibling.

The testing of the brothers is akin to the process of repentance that is central to the Feast of Atonement. Repentance is not merely a matter of feeling guilty or regretful—it involves a transformation of the heart, a change in behavior that demonstrates a commitment to doing what is right. In Joseph's case, he needed to see whether his brothers had truly repented for their betrayal, or if they were still the same men who had sold him into slavery.

In our own lives, the process of repentance is often one that requires self-examination and a willingness to confront the sins of our past. The Feast of Atonement calls us to this kind of introspection, urging us to examine our hearts and to seek forgiveness not only from God but also from those we have wronged. Just as Joseph's brothers were tested to reveal the state of their hearts, we too are called to reflect on the ways we have fallen short and to make amends where necessary.

The Ultimate Test: Judah's Act Of Self-Sacrifice

The ultimate test of the brothers' repentance comes when Joseph arranges for his silver cup to be placed in Benjamin's sack as they prepare to leave Egypt. When the cup is discovered, Joseph declares that Benjamin must remain in Egypt as his slave while the other brothers are free to return home. This moment echoes the earlier betrayal, where the brothers sold Joseph into slavery and returned home without him. Once again, they are faced with a choice: will they abandon Benjamin to save themselves, or will they stand up for him?

It is at this point that Judah, the very brother who had suggested selling Joseph into slavery, steps forward and offers himself as a substitute for Benjamin. In Genesis 44:33, Judah says, "Now then, please let your servant remain here as my lord's slave in place of the boy, and let the boy return with his brothers." This act of self-sacrifice is a profound demonstration of repentance and transformation. Judah, who once led the charge to betray Joseph, now offers his own life to save his brother.

Judah's act of self-sacrifice marks the turning point in the story. It is a powerful moment of reconciliation, where the brothers' past sins are confronted, and the possibility of healing becomes real. In this moment, Joseph knows that his brothers have changed—that they are no longer the men who betrayed him all those years ago. The process of repentance has been completed, and the stage is set for forgiveness and reconciliation.

The theme of substitution and self-sacrifice that we see in Judah's actions is also central to the Feast of Atonement. On Yom Kippur, the high priest would offer a sacrifice on behalf of the people, symbolizing the atonement of their sins and the restoration of their relationship with God. This act of sacrifice pointed forward to the ultimate sacrifice of Christ, who offered Himself as a substitute for us, taking on the penalty of our sins so that we might be reconciled to God. Just as Judah offered himself in place of Benjamin, Christ offers Himself in place of us, securing our forgiveness and restoring our relationship with the Father.

Joseph's Act Of Forgiveness: A Reflection Of

Divine Grace

When Joseph reveals his true identity to his brothers, their reaction is one of shock and fear. They are terrified that Joseph will seek revenge for their betrayal, knowing full well that they deserve punishment. But instead of lashing out in anger, Joseph responds with one of the most powerful statements of forgiveness in all of Scripture: "Do not be distressed or angry with yourselves because you sold me here, for God sent me before you to preserve life" (Genesis 45:5).

Joseph's forgiveness is not just a personal act of mercy—it is a reflection of the divine grace that lies at the heart of the Feast of Atonement. Joseph recognizes that, although his brothers meant to harm him, God had used their actions to bring about a greater good. His ability to see the hand of God at work in his suffering allows him to extend forgiveness to his brothers, releasing them from the guilt and shame of their past actions.

Forgiveness, in the context of the Feast of Atonement, is not simply about letting go of anger or resentment. It is about restoring broken relationships and reestablishing harmony within the community. In Leviticus 16, we see the detailed rituals of the Day of Atonement, where the high priest would offer sacrifices on behalf of the people to cleanse them from their sins and to make atonement for the entire community. This act of atonement was not just about individual forgiveness—it was about the restoration of the people's relationship with God and with one another.

Joseph's forgiveness of his brothers reflects this same principle of communal restoration. By forgiving them, he not only releases them from their guilt but also restores the broken family bond that had been severed by their betrayal. His act of forgiveness paves the way for reconciliation, allowing the family to be reunited and for the promises of God to be fulfilled through them.

The Power Of Reconciliation: A Family Restored

The culmination of Joseph's story is the reconciliation of his family. After revealing his identity and extending forgiveness to his brothers, Joseph invites his entire family to come to Egypt, where he provides for them during the remaining years of the famine. In Genesis 45:9-11, Joseph says, "Hurry and go up to my father and say to him, '"Thus says your son Joseph, 'God has made me lord of all Egypt. Come down to me; do not tarry. You shall dwell in the land of Goshen, and you shall be near me, you and your children and your children's children, and your flocks, your herds, and all that you have. There I will provide for you, for there are yet five years of famine to come, so that you and your household, and all that you have, do not come to poverty.'"

This invitation to dwell in Egypt under Joseph's care is not just a practical arrangement—it is a profound act of reconciliation that mirrors the heart of the Feast of Atonement. The family that was once torn apart by betrayal and jealousy is now being restored. Joseph's willingness to forgive and to provide for his family, even after all that they had done to him, reflects the deep power of reconciliation that comes from God's grace.

In this moment, we see the fulfillment of the dreams that Joseph had as a young boy. His brothers, who once resented him for the dreams of them bowing down to him, now come to him in need, and he welcomes them with open arms. But Joseph's rise to power is not about dominance or control—it is about serving his family and providing for them in their time of need. In this sense, Joseph's story serves as a powerful reflection of the redemptive work of Christ, who uses His power not to condemn but to reconcile us to Himself and to one another.

The reconciliation of Joseph's family is also a foreshadowing of the larger reconciliation that God desires for all of humanity. Just as Joseph's forgiveness restored his family, so too does God's forgiveness, offered through Christ, restore us to right relationship with Him and with each other. The Feast of Atonement points to this ultimate reconciliation—a time when all of creation will be restored, and the broken relationships caused by sin will be healed.

The Feast Of Atonement And The Call To Forgiveness

As we reflect on the themes of forgiveness and reconciliation in Joseph's story, we are reminded of the central message of the Feast of Atonement. This sacred day calls us to examine our hearts, to seek forgiveness for our sins, and to extend forgiveness to those who have wronged us. Just as Joseph tested his brothers and ultimately forgave them, we too are called to go through a process of repentance and forgiveness in our relationships with others.

Forgiveness is not always easy. It requires us to confront the pain of the past and to release our desire for revenge or retribution. But as Joseph's story shows, forgiveness is also a pathway to healing and restoration. By forgiving his brothers, Joseph was not only setting them free from their guilt—he was also setting himself free from the bitterness and resentment that could have consumed him. Forgiveness is a gift, both to the one who receives it and to the one who offers it.

The Feast of Atonement reminds us that forgiveness is not simply a personal choice—it is a divine command. Just as God forgives us through the atoning work of Christ, we are called to forgive others. In Matthew 6:14-15, Jesus says, "For if you forgive other people when they sin against you, your heavenly Father will also forgive you. But if you do not forgive others their sins, your Father will not forgive your sins." Forgiveness is at the heart of the Christian life, and it is through forgiveness that we experience the fullness of God's grace.

Reconciliation And The Kingdom Of God

The story of Joseph and his brothers is not just a personal narrative of family reconciliation—it is a reflection of the larger work of reconciliation that God is doing in the world. Through Christ, God is reconciling all things to Himself, bringing healing to the brokenness caused by sin. In 2 Corinthians 5:18-19, Paul writes, "All this is from God, who through Christ reconciled us to himself and gave us the ministry of reconciliation; that is, in Christ God was reconciling the world to himself, not counting their trespasses against them, and entrusting to us the message of reconciliation."

As followers of Christ, we are called to participate in this ministry of reconciliation. Just as Joseph worked to restore his family, we are called to be agents of reconciliation in a world that is fractured by sin, division, and injustice. This means extending forgiveness to those who have wronged us, seeking peace in our relationships, and working for justice and healing in our communities. The Feast of Atonement reminds us that reconciliation is not just about restoring individual relationships—it is about the restoration of the entire community, and ultimately, the restoration of all creation.

Joseph's story is a powerful example of what this ministry of reconciliation looks like in practice. His willingness to forgive his brothers, to test their hearts, and to restore them to relationship with him reflects the heart of God's work in the world. God is always seeking to restore what has been broken, to heal what has been wounded, and to bring His people back into right relationship with Him and with one another. As we reflect on the themes of the Feast of Atonement, we are reminded that reconciliation is both a gift and a calling—a gift that we receive from God and a calling that we are invited to participate in.

The Feast Of Atonement And The Hope Of Reconciliation

Joseph's story, with its themes of betrayal, repentance, forgiveness, and reconciliation, offers a profound reflection on the meaning of the Feast of Atonement. This sacred day calls us to examine our hearts, to seek forgiveness for our sins, and to work toward the restoration of our relationships with others. In Joseph's journey, we see the power of forgiveness to heal the wounds of the past and to bring about reconciliation in the present.

The Feast of Atonement is not just a ritual—it is a reflection of God's desire for all of creation to be reconciled to Him. Through the atoning work of Christ, we are offered forgiveness and the hope of restoration. Just as Joseph's forgiveness restored his family, Christ's forgiveness restores us to right relationship with God and with one another.

As we celebrate the Feast of Atonement, we are reminded that reconciliation is at the heart of God's redemptive plan. It is through forgiveness that we are healed, and it is through reconciliation that we are made whole. Joseph's story invites us to reflect on the ways in which we can extend forgiveness to those who have wronged us, to seek reconciliation in our relationships, and to participate in the larger work of reconciliation that God is doing in the world.

May we, like Joseph, have the courage to forgive, the wisdom to seek reconciliation, and the grace to be agents of God's healing in a broken world.

Chapter 12: Study Questions For Reflection

The Unveiling of God's Plan—From Hidden to Revealed and *The Feast of Atonement—Forgiveness and Reconciliation*:

1. How does Joseph's story illustrate the way God's plan can remain hidden and gradually unfold over time? Reflect on a time when you experienced a hidden purpose that was later revealed.

2. What lessons can we learn from Joseph's response to his trials regarding faith and trust in God's timing?

3. In what ways do Joseph's early dreams serve as a "glimpse" of God's greater plan for his life? How do they shape his journey despite the challenges he faces?

4. How does the theme of hiddenness in Joseph's life connect to the idea of the Feast of Atonement, where God calls His people to self-examination and reconciliation?

5. Why was it important for Joseph to test his brothers before revealing his identity, and how does this process relate to the deeper purpose of repentance and reconciliation?

6. How does Joseph's forgiveness of his brothers serve as a model for us, especially in light of the themes of the Feast of Atonement? How can we practice forgiveness and reconciliation in our own relationships?

7. Joseph ultimately saw God's hand at work in his suffering and betrayal. How can understanding this perspective help us approach difficult situations in our own lives?

8. How does the concept of the Feast of Atonement deepen our understanding of Joseph's act of forgiveness toward his brothers and their family's

restoration?

CHAPTER 13: RESTORATION OF THE FAMILY—THE SPIRITUAL TEMPLE

The restoration of Joseph's family is one of the most poignant moments in the biblical narrative. It is a story of healing, forgiveness, and reconciliation after years of division, betrayal, and heartache. Yet, beneath the surface of this personal reunion lies a profound spiritual truth: the restoration of Joseph's family foreshadows the greater work of restoration that God is doing in and through His people. This chapter will explore the restoration of Joseph's family as a reflection of the spiritual temple that God is building—a temple not made with human hands, but a community of people restored to one another and to God.

Restoration, both in the biblical sense and in the human experience, is a deeply complex process. It involves not only the mending of broken relationships but also the renewal of identity and purpose. For Joseph and his brothers, the journey toward restoration was not simply a matter of reuniting after years of separation—it was about the healing of wounds that had festered for years, the reconciling of deep-seated resentments, and the reestablishment of a family that would go on to fulfill God's covenant promises. In this sense, their family was more than just a group of individuals—it was a microcosm of the larger story of Israel and the spiritual restoration that God was bringing to His people.

The Family As A Microcosm Of Israel's Restoration

At the heart of Joseph's story is the restoration of his family, a family that would one day form the twelve tribes of Israel. This familial restoration is not just a personal victory for Joseph and his brothers—it is a prophetic foreshadowing of the restoration that God would bring to the entire nation of Israel. Just as Joseph's family was torn apart by sin, betrayal, and jealousy, so too was the nation of Israel fractured by rebellion, idolatry, and disobedience. Yet, just as God worked through Joseph to restore his family, He would one day work through Christ to restore His people.

The twelve sons of Jacob represent more than just a family—they represent the foundation of the nation of Israel. Their reconciliation is symbolic of the greater work of restoration that God would do for the people of Israel. This is particularly significant when we consider the prophetic nature of Joseph's role. As a type of Christ, Joseph's life points forward to the ultimate restoration that Christ would bring—a restoration that goes beyond the physical family of Israel and extends to all who are called to be part of God's spiritual family.

In this way, the restoration of Joseph's family is a precursor to the establishment of the spiritual temple that God is building. The family that was once divided is now reunited, and in their reconciliation, we see a picture of the spiritual reconciliation that God is working among His people. This spiritual temple is not a physical structure but a living community of believers who are being restored to one another and to God through the work of Christ.

The Role Of Forgiveness In Restoration

The restoration of Joseph's family would not have been possible without the profound act of forgiveness that Joseph extended to his brothers. As we explored in the previous chapter, forgiveness is the gateway to reconciliation. Without forgiveness, the wounds of the past remain open, festering and creating barriers to healing. But with forgiveness comes the possibility of restoration—not just of relationships, but of identity, purpose, and hope.

Joseph's forgiveness of his brothers was not a simple or superficial gesture. It came after a long period of testing, during which Joseph discerned whether his brothers had truly repented for their past actions. Once Joseph was assured of their repentance, he was able to offer them the gift of forgiveness—releasing them from the guilt and shame of their betrayal and opening the door to reconciliation.

This act of forgiveness is central to the process of restoration because it reflects the heart of God's work in restoring His people. Just as Joseph forgave his brothers, God extends forgiveness to us, offering us the opportunity to be reconciled to Him and to one another. In 2 Corinthians 5:18-19, Paul writes, "All this is from God, who through Christ reconciled us to himself and gave us the ministry of reconciliation; that is, in Christ God was reconciling the world to himself, not counting their trespasses against them, and entrusting to us the message of reconciliation."

Forgiveness is the foundation upon which restoration is built. Without forgiveness, there can be no true reconciliation, no healing of the divisions that separate us from God and from one another. But when forgiveness is extended—when the past is released and grace is given—the possibility of restoration becomes real. Joseph's story reminds us that forgiveness is not just a personal act of mercy; it is a divine invitation to participate in the larger work of restoration that God is doing in the world.

The Spiritual Temple: A Community Restored

The restoration of Joseph's family is not just about the healing of individual relationships—it is about the restoration of a community. The twelve sons of Jacob represent the twelve tribes of Israel, and their reconciliation foreshadows the gathering of God's people into a spiritual temple—a community of believers who are being built together into a dwelling place for God.

In Ephesians 2:19-22, Paul describes this spiritual temple: "So then you are no longer strangers and aliens, but you are fellow citizens with the saints and members of the household of God, built on the foundation of the apostles and prophets, Christ Jesus himself being the cornerstone, in whom the whole structure, being joined together, grows into a holy temple in the Lord. In him you also are being built together into a dwelling place for God by the Spirit."

This imagery of a spiritual temple reflects the idea that restoration is not just about individual reconciliation with God but about the creation of a new community—a community that is characterized by unity, love, and mutual support. The restoration of Joseph's family is a picture of this larger spiritual reality. Just as Joseph's family was divided and then restored, so too are we, as believers, being restored into a unified community through the work of Christ.

This spiritual temple is not bound by ethnic or national boundaries. It is a global community made up of people from every tribe, tongue, and nation who have been reconciled to God through Christ. The divisions that once separated us—whether they be racial, cultural, or social—are being healed as we are built together into this spiritual temple. In this sense, the restoration of Joseph's family points us toward the ultimate restoration that will take place when Christ returns and gathers His people from all corners of the earth to dwell with Him in perfect unity.

The Role Of Suffering In The Process Of Restoration

The restoration of Joseph's family did not happen without suffering. Joseph's journey from the pit to the palace was marked by years of hardship, betrayal, and injustice. His brothers, too, experienced the suffering of living with the guilt of their actions and the fear of being exposed. Yet, it was through this suffering that God worked to bring about restoration.

Suffering, though painful, is often the means by which God refines us and prepares us for restoration. In Romans 5:3-5, Paul writes, "Not only that, but we rejoice in our sufferings, knowing that suffering produces endurance, and endurance produces character, and character produces hope, and hope does not put us to shame, because God's love has been poured into our hearts through the Holy Spirit who has been given to us." Joseph's story exemplifies this truth. His years of suffering were not wasted—they were the crucible in which his character was forged and his faith was strengthened.

Similarly, Joseph's brothers experienced their own form of suffering, as they wrestled with the guilt of their betrayal and the fear of retribution. Yet, it was through this suffering that they were brought to a place of repentance, where they could finally be reconciled to Joseph and to one another.

In the same way, the process of restoration in our own lives often involves suffering. Whether it be the pain of broken relationships, the weight of unconfessed sin, or the trials of life, suffering has a way of stripping away our pride and self-sufficiency, leading us to a place of humility and dependence on

God. It is often in the midst of suffering that we are most open to the work of restoration, as we recognize our need for God's healing and grace.

The Prophetic Significance Of Restoration In The Life Of Joseph

The restoration of Joseph's family is not just a personal or familial event—it carries deep prophetic significance. In many ways, Joseph's role in restoring his family mirrors the role that Christ plays in restoring humanity to God. Just as Joseph was sent ahead of his family to prepare a place for them during the famine, so too does Christ go ahead of us to prepare a place for us in the kingdom of God.

In John 14:2-3, Jesus tells His disciples, "In my Father's house are many rooms. If it were not so, would I have told you that I go to prepare a place for you? And if I go and prepare a place for you, I will come again and will take you to myself, that where I am you may be also." Joseph's preparation for his family during the famine is a foreshadowing of Christ's preparation for us in the heavenly kingdom. Just as Joseph provided for his family in their time of need, Christ provides for us, both in this life and in the life to come.

Moreover, Joseph's role as a reconciler of his family points to the ultimate work of reconciliation that Christ accomplishes on the cross. Through His death and resurrection, Christ reconciles us to God, healing the division caused by sin and restoring us to right relationship with the Father. In Colossians 1:19-20, Paul writes, "For in him all the fullness of God was pleased to dwell, and through him to reconcile to himself all things, whether on earth or in heaven, making peace by the blood of his cross."

Joseph's story, then, is not just a story of personal restoration—it is a prophetic picture of the greater work of restoration that God is doing in and through Christ. The restoration of Joseph's family points forward to the restoration of all things, when Christ will return to make all things new and to gather His people into the spiritual temple that He is building.

Living In The Hope Of Restoration

As we reflect on the restoration of Joseph's family and its spiritual significance, we are reminded that restoration is at the heart of God's redemptive plan. Just as Joseph's family was restored after years of division and betrayal, so too are we being restored to one another and to God through the work of Christ. This restoration is not just about healing individual relationships—it is about the creation of a new community, a spiritual temple that God is building, in which we are all being united in Christ.

The process of restoration is not always easy. It often involves suffering, repentance, and forgiveness. Yet, as Joseph's story teaches us, the end result is a beautiful picture of reconciliation and healing. God is always at work, restoring what has been broken and bringing us into deeper relationship with Him and with one another.

As we live in the hope of restoration, we are invited to participate in this work of reconciliation. Just as Joseph extended forgiveness to his brothers and worked to restore his family, we are called to be agents of restoration in our own relationships and communities. The spiritual temple that God is building is not complete without us—we are each a part of this living structure, and we are each called to contribute to its growth and unity.

In Joseph's story, we see a glimpse of the larger story of restoration that God is writing in human history—a story that will culminate in the return of Christ and the establishment of His eternal kingdom. As we await that day, may we live in the hope of restoration, trusting that the God who restored Joseph's family is also at work restoring us, building us into a spiritual temple that will one day stand in glory.

Chapter 13: Study Questions For Reflection

Reflecting on Joseph's Life and Trials—A Foreshadowing of the 6th Seal:

1. How does Joseph's journey of betrayal, suffering, and redemption foreshadow the events of the 6th Seal?
2. How can Joseph's example of faithfulness inspire us to endure during times of spiritual testing or hardship?
3. How does Joseph's reconciliation with his brothers reflect God's desire to reconcile with His people?

CHAPTER 14: JOSEPH

A Life of Endurance, Preparation, and Reconciliation

Joseph's life stands as one of the most remarkable stories of endurance, preparation, and reconciliation in all of Scripture. It is a narrative that unfolds over years of hardship, suffering, and injustice, only to culminate in triumph and restoration. The themes of Joseph's life—his ability to endure suffering, his foresight in preparing for the future, and his commitment to reconciliation—serve as powerful lessons not only for understanding his role in God's plan but also for grasping the larger theological truths that his story points to.

In many ways, Joseph's life can be seen as a mirror of the broader human experience. We, too, are often called to endure seasons of difficulty and trial, trusting that God's purposes are being worked out even when we cannot see the end. Like Joseph, we are called to prepare for the future, using the wisdom that God grants us to navigate the uncertainties of life. And, like Joseph, we are called to pursue reconciliation—with God, with one another, and with ourselves—recognizing that restoration and healing are at the heart of God's redemptive plan.

As we reflect on Joseph's life, we will explore how these themes of endurance, preparation, and reconciliation are woven together, not only in Joseph's personal story but also in the larger narrative of Scripture.

Endurance Through Suffering: The Crucible Of Joseph's Faith

At the heart of Joseph's life is the theme of endurance—his ability to remain steadfast and faithful in the face of overwhelming suffering. From the moment his brothers threw him into a pit and sold him into slavery, Joseph's life became a journey marked by hardship and injustice. Yet, throughout it all, Joseph never wavered in his trust in God's faithfulness. His endurance through suffering was not born out of sheer willpower or stoic resignation—it was rooted in a deep conviction that God was with him, even in the darkest moments of his life.

Joseph's early years of suffering, first as a slave in Potiphar's house and then as a prisoner in Pharaoh's dungeon, were not just trials to be endured—they were a crucible in which Joseph's character was forged. These years of hardship shaped Joseph into the leader he would one day become. In many ways, the suffering Joseph endured was a necessary preparation for the responsibilities that lay ahead. Without the experience of suffering, Joseph might not have developed the humility, wisdom, and perseverance that would later define his leadership.

In Genesis 39:21, we read that "the Lord was with Joseph and showed him steadfast love." This simple yet profound statement encapsulates the essence of Joseph's endurance. Despite the injustice he suffered, Joseph was never abandoned by God. In fact, it was precisely in the midst of his suffering that God's presence and favor became most evident. Joseph's ability to endure was not a product of his own strength but a reflection of God's sustaining grace.

The theme of endurance through suffering is one

that resonates deeply with the broader biblical narrative. Throughout Scripture, we see that God often uses suffering to refine and strengthen His people. In Romans 5:3-4, Paul writes, "Not only that, but we rejoice in our sufferings, knowing that suffering produces endurance, and endurance produces character, and character produces hope." Joseph's life is a powerful example of this truth. His suffering produced endurance, which in turn produced the character and wisdom that would later enable him to fulfill his God-given destiny.

For us, Joseph's life serves as a reminder that seasons of suffering are not meaningless. Though we may not always understand why we face certain trials, we can trust that God is at work, using our suffering to shape us into the people He has called us to be. Like Joseph, we are invited to endure with faith, knowing that God's presence is with us, even in the midst of our pain.

Preparation For The Future: The Wisdom Of Foresight

One of the defining aspects of Joseph's life was his ability to prepare for the future. This theme of preparation is most clearly seen in his role as a leader in Egypt, where he was entrusted with the responsibility of managing the nation's resources during a time of abundance and famine. Joseph's wisdom in preparing for the years of famine was not merely the result of his administrative skill—it was a reflection of his God-given ability to discern the times and to act in accordance with God's plan.

The preparation that Joseph oversaw in Egypt was a matter of life and death. Pharaoh's dreams, which Joseph interpreted as a warning of the coming famine, were a divine message that required immediate action. Joseph did not wait for the famine to arrive before he began to prepare. Instead, he used the years of abundance to store up grain, ensuring that there would be enough to sustain the people during the years of scarcity.

In this way, Joseph's preparation for the future can be seen as a model of spiritual discernment and wisdom. He recognized that the present prosperity was not an end in itself but a gift that needed to be stewarded wisely in anticipation of the trials to come. Joseph's foresight and preparation not only saved the nation of Egypt but also provided for the surrounding nations, including his own family.

The theme of preparation is one that carries profound theological significance. In many ways, Joseph's role in preparing for the famine reflects the broader biblical call to be spiritually prepared for the future. Throughout Scripture, we are reminded that this life is not the end, and that we must live in a state of readiness for the return of Christ and the coming of God's kingdom. In Matthew 25:1-13, Jesus tells the parable of the ten virgins, in which five are wise and prepare for the arrival of the bridegroom, while five are foolish and fail to prepare. The message is clear: we are called to be like Joseph, preparing in the present for the future that God has promised.

For us, this preparation involves not only practical wisdom in managing our resources but also spiritual readiness. We are called to cultivate our relationship with God, to grow in our faith, and to steward the gifts and opportunities He has given us in ways that reflect His kingdom values. Like Joseph, we must recognize that the present is a time of preparation, and that how we live now will have lasting implications for the future.

Reconciliation: The Power Of Forgiveness And Healing

Perhaps the most powerful theme in Joseph's life is the theme of reconciliation. After years of betrayal, separation, and suffering, Joseph's story culminates in a remarkable act of forgiveness and reconciliation with his brothers. This moment of reconciliation is not just the resolution of a family drama—it is a profound reflection of the heart of God's redemptive plan for humanity.

When Joseph's brothers first come to Egypt seeking food during the famine, they do not recognize him. But Joseph recognizes them immediately, and rather than revealing his identity right away, he tests them to see if they have truly changed. After several encounters, Joseph finally reveals himself to his brothers, and in that moment, the weight of their betrayal and guilt is lifted. Instead of seeking revenge, Joseph extends forgiveness, saying, "Do not be distressed or angry with yourselves because you sold me here, for God sent me before you to preserve life" (Genesis 45:5).

Joseph's act of forgiveness is a reflection of God's grace and mercy. Despite the wrongs that had been done to him, Joseph chooses to forgive his brothers, recognizing that God had used their actions for a greater purpose. This moment of reconciliation not only restores Joseph's relationship with his brothers but also paves the way for the restoration of their entire family.

The theme of reconciliation in Joseph's story points us to the larger theological truth of God's work of reconciliation in the world. Just as Joseph reconciled with his brothers, God seeks to reconcile us to Himself and to one another. In 2 Corinthians 5:18-19, Paul writes, "All this is from God, who through Christ reconciled us to himself and gave us the ministry of reconciliation; that is, in Christ God was reconciling the world to himself, not counting their trespasses against them, and entrusting to us the message of reconciliation."

Reconciliation is at the heart of God's redemptive plan. Through Christ's death and resurrection, we are offered forgiveness and the opportunity to be restored to right relationship with God. But reconciliation does not stop there—it extends to our relationships with one another. Just as Joseph forgave his brothers and restored their family, we are called to forgive those who have wronged us and to seek reconciliation in our own relationships.

For us, the call to reconciliation is both a gift and a responsibility. It is a gift because we have been forgiven and reconciled to God through Christ. But it is also a responsibility, as we are called to be agents of reconciliation in the world, extending forgiveness and working toward healing in our relationships and communities.

Joseph As A Type Of Christ: Theological Reflections

As we reflect on Joseph's life of endurance, preparation, and reconciliation, it becomes clear that his story is not just a personal narrative of triumph over adversity—it is a prophetic foreshadowing of the life and work of Christ. In many ways, Joseph serves as a type of Christ, pointing us to the ultimate endurance, preparation, and reconciliation that would be accomplished through Jesus.

Like Joseph, Christ endured suffering and betrayal, trusting in the Father's plan even when it led Him to the cross. Both Joseph and Christ were betrayed by those closest to them—Joseph by his brothers, and Christ by Judas, one of His disciples. Yet in both cases, what seemed like a moment of utter defeat became the very means by which God's greater purposes were fulfilled. Just as Joseph's descent into slavery and imprisonment paved the way for his rise to power and the salvation of his family, Christ's descent into death through crucifixion became the means by which He secured the salvation of all humanity.

The parallels between Joseph and Christ do not end with their endurance through suffering. Joseph's role as a provider during the famine, where he used the years of abundance to prepare for the coming crisis, mirrors Christ's role as the provider of spiritual sustenance. Just as Joseph provided physical food to save his family and the surrounding nations from starvation,

Christ offers Himself as the "bread of life," providing eternal sustenance for all who come to Him in faith. In John 6:35, Jesus declares, "I am the bread of life; whoever comes to me shall not hunger, and whoever believes in me shall never thirst." Joseph's provision in the time of famine becomes a prophetic foreshadowing of Christ's provision for our deepest spiritual needs.

Moreover, Joseph's act of reconciliation with his brothers points forward to the ultimate reconciliation that Christ accomplishes between humanity and God. Just as Joseph forgave his brothers, who had wronged him so grievously, Christ extends forgiveness to all who come to Him in repentance. Paul speaks of this reconciliation in Colossians 1:19-20, where he writes, "For in him all the fullness of God was pleased to dwell, and through him to reconcile to himself all things, whether on earth or in heaven, making peace by the blood of his cross." The reconciliation that Joseph brought to his family is a shadow of the much larger reconciliation that Christ brings between humanity and the divine.

The Role Of Divine Providence In Joseph's Life

Another key aspect of Joseph's life that must be highlighted is the theme of divine providence—the understanding that God's hand was at work behind the scenes, orchestrating events for His ultimate purposes. From the moment Joseph was sold into slavery to his rise to power in Egypt, it is clear that God was directing the course of Joseph's life in ways that Joseph himself could not have fully understood at the time.

In Genesis 50:20, Joseph offers one of the most theologically significant statements in the entire Joseph narrative when he says to his brothers, "As for you, you meant evil against me, but God meant it for good, to bring it about that many people should be kept alive, as they are today." This statement reflects a profound understanding of divine providence—the belief that even in the face of human sin and suffering, God is sovereignly working out His purposes for good.

Joseph's recognition of God's providential hand in his life is not simply a retrospective interpretation of events; it is a declaration of faith that invites us to trust in God's goodness even when we cannot see the full picture. Joseph's life teaches us that God's purposes often unfold in ways that we do not expect, and that even in the midst of suffering and hardship, God is working all things together for the good of those who love Him (Romans 8:28).

For us, the theme of divine providence is a source of comfort and hope, especially in times of uncertainty. Like Joseph, we may find ourselves in situations where it seems as though God's plan for our lives has been derailed by the actions of others or by circumstances beyond our control. Yet, Joseph's story reminds us that God's purposes are never thwarted, and that what may seem like a detour or a setback is often part of God's larger plan to bring about redemption and restoration.

The Call To Endurance, Preparation, And Reconciliation

As we reflect on Joseph's life and its theological significance, we are invited to consider how these themes of endurance, preparation, and reconciliation apply to our own lives. Joseph's story is not just a historical narrative—it is a call to live with the same faith, wisdom, and grace that Joseph demonstrated in the face of adversity.

First, we are called to endurance. Just as Joseph endured years of suffering and uncertainty, we too are called to endure the trials of life with faith and perseverance. Endurance is not about denying the reality of suffering—it is about trusting that God is present with us in the midst of our pain and that He is working all things together for our good. As the writer of Hebrews encourages us, "Let us run with endurance the race that is set before us, looking to Jesus, the founder and perfecter of our faith" (Hebrews 12:1-2).

Second, we are called to preparation. Joseph's wisdom in preparing for the years of famine reflects the broader biblical call to live with a sense of spiritual readiness. We do not know what the future holds, but we are called to live in a way that reflects our trust in God's sovereignty and our readiness for the return of Christ. This means stewarding our resources wisely, growing in our faith, and seeking to live in accordance with God's will for our lives. As Jesus said in Matthew 24:44, "Therefore you also must be ready, for the Son of Man is coming at an hour you do not expect."

Finally, we are called to reconciliation. Joseph's act of forgiveness and reconciliation with his brothers is a powerful reminder that we, too, are called to be agents of reconciliation in the world. This begins with accepting the forgiveness that God offers us through Christ, but it extends to our relationships with others. Just as Joseph sought to heal the wounds of the past and restore his family, we are called to seek reconciliation in our own relationships and to work for healing and peace in our communities.

Reconciliation is not always easy—it requires humility, forgiveness, and a willingness to let go of past hurts. But as Joseph's story teaches us, reconciliation is at the heart of God's redemptive plan. Just as God has reconciled us to Himself through Christ, we are called to be ambassadors of reconciliation, extending the grace and forgiveness that we have received to those around us.

A Life Of Endurance, Preparation, And Reconciliation

Joseph's life is a testament to the power of endurance,

the wisdom of preparation, and the transformative grace of reconciliation. Through his story, we see the hand of God at work, orchestrating events for His glory and the good of His people. Joseph's ability to endure suffering, to prepare for the future, and to forgive those who wronged him serves as a model for us as we navigate the challenges of our own lives.

But Joseph's story is not just about personal triumph—it is a prophetic picture of the larger work that God is doing in the world. Through Christ, we see the ultimate fulfillment of the themes that Joseph's life points to. In Christ, we find the endurance to face suffering, the wisdom to prepare for the future, and the grace to be reconciled to God and to one another.

As we live in the light of Joseph's story, we are invited to participate in this larger narrative of redemption. We are called to endure with faith, to prepare with wisdom, and to seek reconciliation with those around us. And as we do, we can trust that the same God who was with Joseph in the pit, the prison, and the palace is with us, working all things together for our good and for His glory.

Chapter 14: Study Questions For Reflection

Joseph—A Life of Endurance, Preparation, and Reconciliation:

1. How does Joseph's life exemplify the need for endurance in times of suffering?
2. What does Joseph's approach to preparation teach us about stewardship?
3. How can reconciliation in Joseph's story inspire reconciliation in our own lives?

CHAPTER 15: REFLECTING ON JOSEPH'S LIFE AND TRIALS—A FORESHADOWING OF THE 6TH SEAL

Joseph's story, filled with betrayal, suffering, endurance, and ultimate vindication, is not merely a historical narrative—it is a powerful foreshadowing of future events that resonate with the eschatological themes found in the Book of Revelation. Among these, the 6th Seal, as described in Revelation 6:12-17, stands out as a period of cosmic upheaval, divine judgment, and ultimate deliverance. In many ways, Joseph's life offers a microcosm of this greater cosmic drama—a reflection of the trials and tribulations that humanity will face, as well as the hope of redemption that lies beyond the tumult.

In this chapter, we will explore how Joseph's personal trials —his betrayal by his brothers, his unjust imprisonment, his years of waiting, and his eventual rise to power—serve as a foreshadowing of the events symbolized by the 6th Seal. We will delve into the deeper theological implications of these connections, considering how Joseph's story can illuminate our understanding of God's unfolding plan in the end times.

Joseph's Betrayal And The Unveiling Of The 6Th Seal: The Beginning Of Sorrows

Joseph's journey of suffering begins with a profound betrayal—his own brothers conspire to strip him of his special status and sell him into slavery. In Genesis 37, we read of how Joseph's brothers, filled with envy and hatred, threw him into a pit and sold him to a caravan of Ishmaelites on their way to Egypt. This act of betrayal marks the first of many trials that Joseph would endure. His descent into slavery is a symbolic "death" of sorts—the death of his favored position in his father's house, the death of his dreams, and the death of his former life.

This moment of betrayal parallels the opening of the 6th Seal in Revelation, where we are introduced to a period of great upheaval and cosmic judgment. The 6th Seal begins with a terrifying vision of natural disasters: a great earthquake, the sun turning black like sackcloth, the moon becoming like blood, and the stars falling from the sky (Revelation 6:12-14). These cosmic signs mark the beginning of what Jesus referred to as the "beginning of sorrows" in Matthew 24:8—a time of tribulation that signals the approaching day of the Lord.

Joseph's betrayal can be seen as a personal "earthquake" in his life—a moment when everything he knew was shaken, and his world was turned upside down. Just as the opening of the 6th Seal brings about a cosmic upheaval, Joseph's betrayal brings about a personal upheaval that would set him on a path of suffering and trial. The pit into which Joseph was thrown symbolizes the darkness and uncertainty that often accompanies the initial stages of tribulation—whether on a personal or cosmic scale.

Yet, even in this moment of betrayal, God's hand is at work, guiding Joseph toward a greater purpose. This theme of divine sovereignty in the midst of suffering is echoed in the events of the 6th Seal. While the natural disasters and cosmic signs may seem chaotic and terrifying, they are ultimately part of God's plan to bring about the redemption of His people. Just as Joseph's descent into slavery was the beginning of a journey that would ultimately lead to his rise to power, the events of the 6th Seal are part of a larger plan that will culminate in the establishment of God's kingdom on earth.

Joseph's Imprisonment And The Time Of Testing: Parallels To The 6Th Seal's Tribulation

After being sold into slavery, Joseph's trials continued. He was purchased by Potiphar, a high-ranking official in Egypt, and for a time, it seemed as though Joseph's fortunes were improving. However, when Joseph was falsely accused by Potiphar's wife of attempting to assault her, he was thrown into prison—a place of isolation, suffering, and waiting. Joseph's imprisonment can be seen as a time of testing—a period during which his faith in God's promises was refined and strengthened.

This time of testing parallels the tribulation associated with the 6th Seal. In Revelation 6:15-17, we read that as the cosmic signs unfold, "the kings of the earth, the princes, the generals, the rich, the mighty, and everyone else, both slave and free, hid in caves and among the rocks of the mountains." These individuals, confronted with the reality of God's judgment, cry out in fear, seeking to hide from the wrath of the Lamb. This moment of fear and hiding reflects the intense trial and testing that will accompany the unfolding of God's plan in the end times.

Joseph's imprisonment, like the tribulation of the 6th Seal, was a period of intense testing. Cut off from his family, his homeland, and the life he once knew, Joseph could easily have given in to despair. Yet, throughout his time in prison, Joseph remained steadfast in his trust in God's promises. Even in the darkest moments, Joseph believed that God had a plan for his life—a plan that would eventually be revealed.

In the same way, the tribulation of the 6th Seal is a time when believers are called to endure, trusting that God's plan is unfolding even in the midst of chaos and suffering. The fear and trembling that accompany the cosmic signs of the 6th Seal are not the end of the story—just as Joseph's time in prison was not the end of his story. Instead, these trials serve as a prelude to the ultimate deliverance and restoration that God has promised.

The Revelation Of Joseph's Identity And The Unveiling Of The Lamb: The Moment Of Revelation

One of the most dramatic moments in Joseph's story comes when he reveals his true identity to his brothers. After testing their hearts and seeing that they had repented for their earlier betrayal, Joseph reveals himself, declaring, "I am Joseph, your brother, whom you sold into Egypt!" (Genesis 45:4). This moment of revelation is both a moment of judgment—Joseph's brothers are confronted with the reality of their sin—and a moment of grace, as Joseph extends forgiveness and offers them a place of refuge in Egypt.

This moment of revelation parallels the unveiling of the Lamb in Revelation 6. Just as Joseph revealed his identity to his brothers, so too does the Lamb—Jesus Christ—reveal Himself in His glory and power during the events of the 6th Seal. In Revelation 6:16-17, those who witness the cosmic signs cry out, "Fall on us and hide us from the face of him who sits on the throne and from the wrath of the Lamb! For the great day of their wrath has come, and who can stand?"

This moment of revelation is both awe-inspiring and

terrifying. Just as Joseph's brothers were filled with fear when they realized who he was, so too will humanity be filled with fear when they come face-to-face with the reality of God's judgment. Yet, just as Joseph's revelation to his brothers was accompanied by an offer of forgiveness and reconciliation, the unveiling of the Lamb is not solely about judgment—it is also about the offer of salvation to those who repent and turn to Christ.

In Joseph's story, the revelation of his identity leads to the reconciliation of his family. His brothers, who once betrayed him, are now brought into a place of refuge and provision in Egypt. In the same way, the unveiling of the Lamb in Revelation offers the hope of reconciliation and salvation to all who repent and seek refuge in Christ. The 6th Seal, with its signs of cosmic upheaval, is not merely a warning of impending doom—it is an invitation to turn to the Lamb and find salvation in His sacrifice.

The Restoration Of Joseph's Family And The Gathering Of God's People: The Fulfillment Of The 6Th Seal's Promise

The culmination of Joseph's story is the restoration of his family. After years of separation, betrayal, and suffering, Joseph's brothers come to Egypt seeking food during the famine, and it is there that they are reunited with their long-lost brother. Through Joseph's forgiveness and provision, the family is restored, and they are given a place of refuge in the land of Goshen.

This moment of restoration mirrors the gathering of God's people that is foreshadowed in the 6th Seal. In Revelation, the opening of the 6th Seal marks a turning point in the cosmic drama of the end times—a moment when the final judgment draws near, but also a moment when God's people are gathered and protected. In Revelation 7, immediately following the events of the 6th Seal, we see the sealing of the 144,000 from the tribes of Israel, as well as the great multitude from every nation, tribe, people, and language standing before the throne of God, clothed in white robes and holding palm branches (Revelation 7:9).

The restoration of Joseph's family is a picture of this final gathering—a time when the divisions and betrayals of the past are healed, and God's people are brought together in unity and peace. Just as Joseph's family was given a place of refuge in Egypt, so too will God's people find refuge in His presence, sheltered from the tribulation and judgment that are to come.

The story of Joseph, then, is not just a tale of personal redemption—it is a foreshadowing of the ultimate reconciliation and restoration that God will bring to all creation. Joseph's family, torn apart by betrayal and sin, is restored in a place of refuge, just as God's people—estranged from Him by sin—are ultimately restored and reconciled through Christ. In both stories, the outcome is not simply survival but the flourishing of a community of people brought into fellowship and peace.

In this way, Joseph's life points beyond itself, offering a glimpse into the unfolding plan of God, where redemption is not just personal but cosmic, where individual lives reflect broader spiritual truths. As Joseph's story moves toward its conclusion with his family restored and thriving in Egypt, we are reminded that this reconciliation is but a precursor to the ultimate restoration that God will accomplish through Christ in the end times. Just as Joseph's forgiveness healed the wounds of his family, so too will Christ's return bring about the healing of all creation, reconciling all things to Himself and establishing His kingdom of peace and justice.

The 6Th Seal And The Promise Of Redemption

The 6th Seal in the Book of Revelation signals a dramatic moment in the unfolding of God's eschatological plan. It marks the point at which the final judgment looms near, and yet, it is also a prelude to the full revelation of God's redemptive purposes. The chaos and destruction described in the 6th Seal —the great earthquake, the darkened sun, the blood-red moon —are not simply signs of doom; they are signs of transition, heralding the arrival of God's kingdom.

Joseph's life, with its dramatic twists of fate, also reflects this theme of transition. Each moment of suffering and hardship, from the pit to the prison, was not an end but a transition to a new stage in God's plan. Similarly, the events of the 6th Seal are not the end of the story. They are the beginning of the final stages of God's redemptive plan, when judgment and salvation are revealed in their fullness.

For believers, the 6th Seal is both a warning and a promise. It is a warning of the trials and tribulations that will come, but it is also a promise that those who endure will see the fulfillment of God's purposes. Just as Joseph endured years of suffering before seeing the fulfillment of God's promises in his life, so too are we called to endure, trusting that God's plan is unfolding even in the midst of chaos and uncertainty.

In Revelation 7, we see the sealing of the 144,000, a symbolic representation of God's protection over His people during the time of tribulation. This sealing is a reminder that, just as God protected and provided for Joseph during his years of trial, He will protect and provide for His people during the end times. The events of the 6th Seal, while terrifying in their scope, are not a cause for despair but a call to trust in God's sovereignty and to place our hope in His promises.

Endurance, Preparation, And The Hope Of Restoration

As we reflect on the life of Joseph and its parallels to the 6th Seal, one of the most striking themes is the call to endurance.

Joseph's life was a long journey of endurance through trials, betrayal, and suffering, yet at every stage, God was with him, guiding him toward a greater purpose. Joseph's endurance was not passive resignation—it was an active trust in the goodness and faithfulness of God, even when the circumstances seemed hopeless.

The 6th Seal, with its apocalyptic imagery, also calls believers to endurance. The cosmic signs and tribulations described in Revelation 6 are meant to shake the foundations of the world, but they are also meant to refine the faith of God's people. As Jesus said in Matthew 24:13, "But the one who endures to the end will be saved." The events of the 6th Seal are a reminder that, just as Joseph's life was marked by endurance through suffering, so too are we called to endure, trusting that God's plan is being fulfilled even in the midst of tribulation.

Joseph's preparation for the years of famine also offers a model for how we are to live in the time of waiting before the fulfillment of God's eschatological plan. Just as Joseph used the years of abundance to store up grain and prepare for the famine, we are called to use the time we have now to prepare spiritually for the trials that may come. This preparation involves cultivating our relationship with God, growing in faith and trust, and living in accordance with His will. The events of the 6th Seal remind us that the time is short, and we must be ready, not just for the trials that may come, but for the ultimate restoration that God has promised.

Joseph's story also reminds us of the power of reconciliation. His ability to forgive his brothers and restore his family is a reflection of the greater reconciliation that God is working in the world through Christ. Just as Joseph's forgiveness brought healing to his family, Christ's sacrifice on the cross brings reconciliation between humanity and God, healing the division caused by sin and offering us the hope of eternal life.

The 6th Seal, with its signs of judgment and cosmic upheaval, may seem to emphasize destruction, but it is also a reminder of the reconciliation and restoration that God is bringing to all creation. Just as Joseph's life culminated in the restoration of his family, the events of the 6th Seal point forward to the ultimate restoration of all things, when God's kingdom will be fully established, and His people will dwell with Him in peace and righteousness.

The Unfolding Of God's Plan Through Joseph And The 6Th Seal

As we come to the conclusion of Joseph's story, we see how his life serves as a powerful foreshadowing of the events described in the 6th Seal of Revelation. Joseph's betrayal, suffering, endurance, and ultimate reconciliation with his family reflect the broader themes of tribulation, judgment, and redemption that are central to the unfolding of God's eschatological plan.

Joseph's life teaches us that God's purposes are often hidden in the midst of suffering, but they are always moving toward redemption and restoration. Just as Joseph's journey from the pit to the palace was part of God's plan to save his family and the nations, so too are the events of the 6th Seal part of God's plan to bring about the final redemption of His people and the restoration of creation.

For us, Joseph's story is an invitation to trust in God's sovereignty, even when the world seems to be falling apart. It is a reminder that endurance through trials is not in vain, and that reconciliation and restoration are at the heart of God's redemptive plan. As we reflect on the parallels between Joseph's life and the 6th Seal, we are reminded that the trials we face are not the end of the story—they are part of a larger narrative of hope, redemption, and the ultimate fulfillment of God's promises.

Just as Joseph's life culminated in the restoration of his family, so too will the events of the 6th Seal culminate in the restoration of all things. The cosmic signs, the tribulation, and the judgment are not the final word—God's plan is one of reconciliation and renewal. And as we await the final fulfillment of that plan, we are called to live with endurance, preparation, and hope, trusting that the same God who was with Joseph in the pit, the prison, and the palace is with us now, guiding us toward the ultimate restoration that He has promised.

Chapter 15: Study Questions For Reflection

The Role of Faith Amidst Tribulations:

1. How does Joseph's faith sustain him throughout his trials?
2. In what ways does Joseph's endurance foreshadow the endurance needed by believers?

PART 3: THE DELIVERER AND THE PRESERVER—JOSEPH AS A TYPE OF CHRIST

CHAPTER 16: JOSEPH AS A FORESHADOWING OF THE MESSIAH'S ROLE IN DELIVERANCE AND PRESERVATION

Throughout Joseph's life, we see the recurring theme of deliverance. Joseph's journey from betrayal and imprisonment to becoming the second-in-command of Egypt is not only a story of personal survival—it is a narrative of God's sovereign hand working to preserve life on a much grander scale. As we examine Joseph's role in delivering both Egypt and his own family from the devastation of famine, we begin to see a deeper prophetic connection to the Messiah's work of spiritual deliverance. Just as Joseph was sent ahead to preserve life, the Messiah comes as the ultimate Deliverer, providing salvation and preserving humanity from spiritual death.

In this chapter, we will explore how Joseph's role in the physical deliverance of Egypt and Israel serves as a foreshadowing of Christ's role in the spiritual deliverance of all humanity. We will also reflect on how Joseph's wisdom in preparing for the years of famine points to the Messiah's ongoing work of preserving and sustaining His people through trials, offering a message of hope and endurance for believers today.

Joseph's Role As A Deliverer: Preserving Life In The Face Of Famine

One of the most striking aspects of Joseph's life is the pivotal role he plays in delivering both Egypt and his family from the devastating effects of famine. After interpreting Pharaoh's dreams and foreseeing the seven years of abundance followed by seven years of famine, Joseph is appointed to oversee the collection and storage of grain during the years of plenty. His wisdom and foresight ensure that Egypt is prepared when the famine strikes, and because of his leadership, Egypt becomes a place of refuge not only for its own people but also for those from surrounding nations.

In Genesis 41:56-57, we read, "When the famine had spread over the whole country, Joseph opened all the storehouses and sold grain to the Egyptians, for the famine was severe throughout Egypt. And all the world came to Egypt to buy grain from Joseph, because the famine was severe everywhere." Joseph's role as a provider and sustainer during this time of crisis elevates him from a mere administrator to a figure of salvation, a man through whom God's deliverance flows.

This role of deliverance points to a deeper prophetic connection with the Messiah. Just as Joseph was sent ahead to provide for the physical needs of those suffering from famine, Christ is sent into the world to meet the spiritual needs of humanity. In John 6:35, Jesus declares, "I am the bread of life. Whoever comes to me will never go hungry, and whoever believes in me will never be thirsty." Joseph's distribution of physical bread during the famine foreshadows Christ's offer of spiritual sustenance—eternal life through faith in Him.

In both cases, the deliverance offered is not temporary but comprehensive. Joseph's provision of grain sustains life through a period of crisis, just as Christ's offer of Himself as the bread of life provides eternal sustenance for those who believe. The famine that struck Egypt was devastating, but it was limited to a season. In contrast, the spiritual famine that Christ addresses—humanity's separation from God because of sin—is an eternal condition unless remedied by the deliverance He provides.

The Messianic Pattern Of Preservation: Joseph And Christ As Providers Of Refuge

Joseph's role as a preserver of life extends beyond mere survival. His leadership not only saves Egypt but also creates a place of refuge for his own family. When Jacob and his sons run out of food in Canaan, they journey to Egypt, seeking relief. Unbeknownst to them, it is Joseph—the very brother they betrayed—who holds their future in his hands. In a profound act of grace and forgiveness, Joseph provides for his family, inviting them to live in the land of Goshen where they will be sustained throughout the remaining years of famine.

This act of preserving and providing refuge for his family mirrors the Messiah's work of preserving His people. In the same way that Joseph created a place of physical safety and sustenance for his family, Christ creates a spiritual refuge for all who come to Him. In Matthew 11:28-30, Jesus invites, "Come to me, all you who are weary and burdened, and I will give you rest. Take my yoke upon you and learn from me, for I am gentle and humble in heart, and you will find rest for your souls."

The land of Goshen, where Joseph's family was sheltered during the famine, serves as a symbolic foreshadowing of the spiritual refuge that Christ offers. Just as Joseph's family was protected from the ravages of famine in Goshen, believers are protected from the ultimate consequences of sin and death through Christ's provision. The Messiah's role as a preserver of life goes beyond mere survival—He offers rest, peace, and security in the midst of life's storms.

Moreover, just as Joseph was sent ahead of his family to prepare a place for them, Christ tells His disciples in John 14:2-3, "My Father's house has many rooms; if that were not so, would I have told you that I am going there to prepare a place for you? And if I go and prepare a place for you, I will come back and take you to be with me that you also may be where I am." Joseph's actions in preparing a refuge for his family serve as a prophetic shadow of Christ's work in preparing an eternal home for His people.

Foresight And Preparation: Joseph's Wisdom And The Messiah's Call To Spiritual Readiness

Another key aspect of Joseph's role as a deliverer is his wisdom in preparing for the future. Joseph's interpretation of Pharaoh's dreams gave him insight into the coming famine, and his careful management of Egypt's resources ensured that the nation would be ready when the famine struck. This wisdom in preparing for future hardship is not merely an administrative skill—it is a reflection of Joseph's ability to discern God's plan and to act accordingly.

In the same way, Christ calls His followers to be spiritually prepared for the trials and tribulations that will come. In Matthew 25, Jesus tells the parable of the ten virgins, five of whom were wise and prepared for the arrival of the bridegroom, while five were foolish and unprepared. The message of the parable is clear: just as Joseph prepared Egypt for the famine, we too must be spiritually prepared for the return of Christ and the fulfillment of God's kingdom.

Joseph's preparation was not simply for his own survival—it was for the survival of many. In the same way, the Messiah's call to spiritual readiness is not just for our personal benefit—it is a call to be prepared to serve others, to be ready to offer the spiritual sustenance that Christ provides to those who are in need. In 1 Peter 3:15, believers are exhorted to "always be prepared to give an answer to everyone who asks you to give the reason for the hope that you have."

Joseph's preparation during the years of abundance ensured that Egypt had enough to feed not only its own people but also those from surrounding nations who came seeking relief. In the same way, Christ's followers are called to be spiritually prepared to offer hope and sustenance to those who are lost and searching. Our spiritual readiness, like Joseph's preparation, is not just for our own benefit—it is part of God's larger plan to bring deliverance to all who seek Him.

Joseph's Acts Of Reconciliation And Christ's Work Of Redemption

One of the most powerful aspects of Joseph's story is his decision to reconcile with the very brothers who had betrayed him. After testing their hearts and seeing that they had truly repented, Joseph reveals his identity and extends forgiveness, saying, "Do not be afraid. Am I in the place of God? You intended to harm me, but God intended it for good to accomplish what is now being done, the saving of many lives" (Genesis 50:19-20).

This act of reconciliation is a profound foreshadowing of Christ's work of redemption. Just as Joseph forgave his brothers and restored them to a place of favor, Christ offers forgiveness and restoration to all who come to Him in repentance. In Colossians 1:19-20, Paul writes, "For God was pleased to have all his fullness dwell in him, and through him to reconcile to himself all things, whether things on earth or things in heaven, by making peace through his blood, shed on the cross."

The reconciliation that Joseph brought to his family is a microcosm of the greater reconciliation that Christ brings to all of creation. Joseph's ability to see God's hand at work in the midst of his suffering allowed him to extend forgiveness to his brothers, just as Christ, in His perfect obedience to the Father's will, extends forgiveness to all who turn to Him. Joseph's life, then, becomes a prophetic picture of the redemptive work of Christ, who, through His death and resurrection, reconciles humanity to God and brings about the ultimate deliverance from sin and death.

The Messiah As The Ultimate Deliverer And Preserver

As we reflect on Joseph's life and its prophetic connections, we see that Joseph's role as a deliverer and preserver of life during the famine points to the greater work of the Messiah. Just as Joseph was sent ahead to provide for Egypt and his family, Christ is sent into the world to provide for our deepest spiritual needs. Joseph's wisdom in preparing for the famine, his acts of reconciliation, and his role in preserving life all serve as foreshadowings of the Messiah's work of salvation and preservation.

Through Joseph's story, we are reminded that God's plan of deliverance is not limited to physical survival—it encompasses the spiritual restoration and preservation of His people. The Messiah's role as the bread of life, the provider of refuge, and the reconciler of all things is the ultimate fulfillment of the patterns we see in Joseph's life. As we continue to reflect on these prophetic connections, we are invited to trust in the Messiah's provision, to prepare ourselves spiritually, and to participate in the work of reconciliation and deliverance that Christ is bringing to the world.

Chapter 16: Study Questions For Reflection

Divine Wisdom in Leadership:
1. What role does divine wisdom play in Joseph's rise to power?
2. How can we apply Joseph's reliance on divine wisdom to our daily lives?

CHAPTER 17: JOSEPH AND THE SOVEREIGNTY OF GOD

A Foreshadowing of Christ's Kingship and Dominion

Joseph's ascent to power in Egypt is not just a story of personal triumph—it is a narrative that showcases the sovereignty of God, a sovereignty that is ultimately expressed in the kingship and dominion of Christ. Joseph's journey from a pit to the palace is a remarkable example of God's providential hand at work, shaping events not only for the preservation of a nation but also to reveal His divine plan for all of creation. In Joseph's role as a ruler in Egypt, we find a prophetic foreshadowing of the kingship of Christ, the one who will rule over all nations with justice, wisdom, and authority.

In this chapter, we will explore how Joseph's rise to power points to Christ's role as King and sovereign Lord. We will reflect on how Joseph's authority in Egypt mirrors the Messiah's ultimate dominion, and how both figures embody the divine truth that God's plans are not thwarted by human actions but are fulfilled in His perfect timing.

The Sovereignty Of God In Joseph's Rise To Power

Joseph's life is a testament to the sovereignty of God, a theme that runs throughout the biblical narrative. From the moment Joseph is sold into slavery by his brothers, it becomes clear that, though human hands intended evil, God's purposes were being worked out behind the scenes. Joseph himself recognizes this truth in Genesis 50:20, when he tells his brothers, "You intended to harm me, but God intended it for good to accomplish what is now being done, the saving of many lives." This statement reflects a profound understanding of God's sovereignty—the belief that, despite human intentions and actions, God's will ultimately prevails.

Joseph's rise to power in Egypt is a dramatic example of how God orchestrates events for His purposes. After years of suffering and imprisonment, Joseph is suddenly elevated to the second-highest position in the most powerful nation in the world. Pharaoh recognizes Joseph's unique ability to interpret dreams and his wisdom in managing the impending crisis of famine, and he appoints Joseph to oversee the entire land of Egypt. In Genesis 41:40-41, Pharaoh says to Joseph, "You shall be over my house, and all my people shall order themselves as you command. Only as regards the throne will I be greater than you." This moment marks a dramatic shift in Joseph's life—he goes from being a prisoner to a ruler in the blink of an eye, a transformation that can only be attributed to the sovereign hand of God.

Joseph's rise to power is not simply a story of personal vindication—it is a prophetic foreshadowing of the ultimate reign of Christ, the one who is exalted above all rulers and powers. Just as Joseph was given authority over the land of Egypt, Christ is given authority over all creation. In Philippians

2:9-11, Paul writes, "Therefore God has highly exalted him and bestowed on him the name that is above every name, so that at the name of Jesus every knee should bow, in heaven and on earth and under the earth, and every tongue confess that Jesus Christ is Lord, to the glory of God the Father." The sovereignty that Joseph exercised in Egypt is a reflection of the greater sovereignty that Christ will exercise over all nations and all creation.

Joseph's Authority And Christ's Kingship

The authority that Joseph wielded in Egypt was not his own —it was given to him by Pharaoh, who recognized that Joseph's wisdom came from God. In Genesis 41:38, Pharaoh says, "Can we find anyone like this man, one in whom is the spirit of God?" Joseph's authority was a delegated authority, entrusted to him because of his unique ability to discern God's plan and to act in accordance with it. In this way, Joseph's authority foreshadows the authority of Christ, who is the ultimate embodiment of divine wisdom and truth.

Christ's authority, however, is not delegated—it is inherent. As the Son of God, Christ possesses all authority in heaven and on earth. In Matthew 28:18, after His resurrection, Jesus declares to His disciples, "All authority in heaven and on earth has been given to me." This authority is not limited to a specific nation or time period—it is universal and eternal. Just as Joseph's authority extended over all of Egypt, Christ's authority extends over all creation. He is the King of kings and the Lord of lords, the one who rules with justice, wisdom, and compassion.

Joseph's role as a ruler in Egypt also points to the nature of Christ's kingship. Joseph was not a tyrant—he ruled with wisdom and integrity, using his power to preserve life and to provide for those in need. His rule was characterized by justice and mercy, qualities that reflect the nature of Christ's reign. In Isaiah 9:6-7, the prophet describes the Messiah's rule in these terms: "For to us a child is born, to us a son is given, and the government will be on his shoulders. And he will be called Wonderful Counselor, Mighty God, Everlasting Father, Prince of Peace. Of the greatness of his government and peace there will be no end. He will reign on David's throne and over his kingdom, establishing and upholding it with justice and righteousness from that time on and forever."

Just as Joseph's rule brought peace and provision to Egypt, Christ's reign will bring peace and righteousness to all creation. His kingdom is not one of oppression but of justice, mercy, and love. The kingship of Christ is the fulfillment of the pattern we see in Joseph's life—a ruler who is wise, compassionate, and just, and who uses His authority to bring about the flourishing of His people.

Joseph's Wisdom And Christ's Eternal Dominion

One of the defining characteristics of Joseph's rule in Egypt was his wisdom. Joseph's ability to interpret dreams and to manage the resources of Egypt during the years of famine was a testament to his God-given wisdom. Pharaoh recognized this wisdom and entrusted Joseph with the task of overseeing the nation's survival during a time of crisis. Joseph's wisdom not only saved Egypt but also extended to the surrounding nations, who came to Egypt to buy grain during the famine.

This theme of wisdom as a key aspect of Joseph's rule points to the ultimate wisdom of Christ, who is described in Scripture as the "wisdom of God" (1 Corinthians 1:24). Just as Joseph's wisdom preserved the lives of many, Christ's wisdom brings eternal life to all who believe in Him. In Colossians 2:3, Paul writes that in Christ "are hidden all the treasures of wisdom and knowledge." The wisdom that Joseph displayed in managing the famine is a shadow of the infinite wisdom that Christ possesses as the eternal King.

Moreover, Joseph's role in preserving life during the famine points to Christ's role in preserving and sustaining His people. Just as Joseph stored up grain during the years of abundance to provide for the years of famine, Christ provides spiritual sustenance for His people, sustaining them through times of trial and tribulation. In John 6:35, Jesus declares, "I am the bread of life. Whoever comes to me will never go hungry, and whoever believes in me will never be thirsty." Joseph's wisdom in providing physical sustenance during the famine is a prophetic picture of Christ's provision of spiritual sustenance for His followers.

The wisdom of Joseph, however, was limited to his role in Egypt and to the specific crisis of the famine. In contrast, the wisdom of Christ is eternal and universal. Christ's wisdom is not limited to a particular time or place—it is the wisdom that governs all creation and that will be fully revealed in the new heavens and the new earth. In Revelation 11:15, we read, "The kingdom of the world has become the kingdom of our Lord and of his Christ, and he will reign for ever and ever." The dominion of Christ is eternal, and His wisdom will guide the redeemed creation for all eternity.

The Prophetic Connection: Joseph's Reign And Christ's Sovereignty

The connection between Joseph's reign in Egypt and Christ's sovereignty over all creation is a profound one. Joseph's journey from the pit to the palace is a story of divine providence and sovereignty, a story that points to the greater reality of Christ's kingship. Just as Joseph's rule brought peace, provision, and justice to Egypt, Christ's reign will bring peace, righteousness, and life to all creation.

In Joseph, we see a glimpse of the Messiah's role as the King who rules with wisdom, justice, and compassion. We see a foreshadowing of the one who will one day establish His kingdom on earth, a kingdom where every knee will bow and every tongue will confess that He is Lord. The sovereignty of God, as revealed in Joseph's life, is a reminder that God's plans are not thwarted by human actions or circumstances. Just as God worked through Joseph's trials and triumphs to bring about His purposes, so too is He working through the unfolding of history to bring about the ultimate reign of Christ.

Christ's Kingship And The Hope Of Restoration

As we reflect on Joseph's life and its prophetic connection to the kingship of Christ, we are reminded of the hope that comes with the knowledge of God's sovereignty. Joseph's rise to power was not just a story of personal success—it was a testimony to the sovereign hand of God, a hand that is at work in all of history, guiding events toward the fulfillment of His purposes.

Just as Joseph's rule brought peace and provision to Egypt, Christ's reign will bring peace, justice, and restoration to all creation. The kingship of Christ is the ultimate fulfillment of the pattern we see in Joseph's life—a ruler who is wise, compassionate, and just, and who uses His authority to bring about the flourishing of His people.

As we look forward to the return of Christ and the establishment of His eternal kingdom, we can take comfort in the knowledge that, just as God was sovereign over Joseph's life, He is sovereign over all creation. The rise of Joseph to power foreshadows the greater reign of Christ, the one who is the King of kings and the Lord of lords, and who will reign forever and ever.

Chapter 17: Study Questions For Reflection

Forgiveness as a Path to Reconciliation:
1. Why does Joseph test his brothers before fully reconciling with them?
2. How does Joseph's forgiveness reflect God's forgiveness toward humanity?

CHAPTER 18: JOSEPH AND THE REVERSAL OF FORTUNE

A Prophetic Picture of Resurrection and New Life

The life of Joseph is marked by one of the most dramatic reversals of fortune in all of Scripture. Betrayed by his own brothers, thrown into a pit, sold into slavery, and later imprisoned under false accusations, Joseph's descent into suffering seems, at times, to be without hope. And yet, at the moment when all seems lost, God's sovereign hand intervenes, lifting Joseph from the depths of the dungeon to the heights of power in Egypt. His rise from despair to authority is not just a personal victory—it is a profound picture of the redemptive work of God, a foreshadowing of the ultimate reversal of fortune found in Christ's resurrection.

In this chapter, we will explore how Joseph's journey from the pit to power prophetically mirrors Christ's death and resurrection. Just as Joseph was lifted from imprisonment to rule over Egypt, so too was Christ raised from the dead to reign as the eternal King. We will also reflect on how Joseph's story points to the hope of resurrection and new life for believers, offering a vision of God's power to redeem and restore what has been broken.

From The Pit To The Palace: Joseph's Descent And Ascent

The story of Joseph's descent into the pit is a familiar one, filled with pain and betrayal. His brothers, motivated by jealousy and hatred, conspire to rid themselves of Joseph by throwing him into a cistern and later selling him to a group of passing traders. This act of treachery marks the beginning of a long and painful journey for Joseph—a journey that takes him from the heights of being his father's favored son to the depths of slavery and imprisonment.

Joseph's time in the pit and his subsequent imprisonment can be seen as symbolic of death. The pit, in particular, represents a place of abandonment and despair, where Joseph's dreams of greatness seem to have come to a tragic end. Likewise, his unjust imprisonment in Egypt further deepens the sense of isolation and loss. In many ways, Joseph's life appears to be over—his hopes of fulfilling the dreams given to him by God have been shattered, and his future seems bleak.

But Joseph's story does not end in the pit. Just as quickly as Joseph was thrown into despair, he is lifted up by the hand of God. Through a series of divinely orchestrated events, Joseph is brought to the attention of Pharaoh, who elevates him to the second-highest position in Egypt. Joseph's ascent from the dungeon to the palace is a powerful reversal of fortune, one that highlights God's ability to bring life out of death, hope out of despair.

This dramatic reversal in Joseph's life serves as a prophetic foreshadowing of the resurrection of Christ. Just as Joseph was lifted from the depths of the pit, so too was Christ raised from the dead after His crucifixion. In Philippians 2:8-9, Paul writes, "And being found in appearance as a man, he humbled himself by becoming obedient to death—even death on a cross! Therefore God exalted him to the highest place and gave him the name that is above every name." The resurrection of Christ is the ultimate reversal of fortune, the moment when death is defeated and new life is made possible for all who believe.

Joseph's Rise To Power And The Resurrection Of Christ

Joseph's rise to power in Egypt is not just a personal vindication—it is a sign of God's sovereign plan for the salvation of many. After interpreting Pharaoh's dreams and predicting the coming famine, Joseph is placed in charge of all the resources of Egypt. His position of authority allows him to save not only Egypt but also the surrounding nations from the devastation of famine. In Genesis 41:40-41, Pharaoh says to Joseph, "You shall be over my house, and all my people shall order themselves as you command. Only as regards the throne will I be greater than you."

This moment of exaltation mirrors Christ's resurrection and ascension to the right hand of God. Just as Joseph was given authority over the land of Egypt, Christ is given authority over all creation. In Matthew 28:18, Jesus declares, "All authority in heaven and on earth has been given to me." Christ's resurrection is not merely a return to life—it is a declaration of His victory over sin and death, and His exaltation as King of kings and Lord of lords. The resurrection is the ultimate act of God's power to reverse the curse of sin and death, bringing new life to all who place their faith in Christ.

Joseph's rise to power also points to the redemptive purpose of Christ's resurrection. Just as Joseph's exaltation was part of God's plan to preserve life during the famine, Christ's resurrection is part of God's plan to offer eternal life to all who believe. In

1 Corinthians 15:22, Paul writes, "For as in Adam all die, so in Christ all will be made alive." The resurrection is not just a reversal of Christ's own death—it is the beginning of a new creation, a new reality in which death no longer has the final word.

The Prophetic Hope Of Resurrection And New Life For Believers

Joseph's reversal of fortune is not only a picture of Christ's resurrection—it is also a prophetic promise of the new life that is available to all who trust in God. Just as Joseph was raised from the pit and exalted to a position of authority, believers are promised that they too will share in the resurrection and reign of Christ. In Romans 6:4, Paul writes, "We were therefore buried with him through baptism into death in order that, just as Christ was raised from the dead through the glory of the Father, we too may live a new life."

The resurrection is the ultimate reversal of fortune for humanity. Through Christ's death and resurrection, the curse of sin is broken, and the promise of eternal life is made available to all who believe. Just as Joseph's life was redeemed and restored after years of suffering, so too are believers promised that their lives will be redeemed and restored through the power of Christ's resurrection.

In Joseph's story, we see a glimpse of this future hope. His rise to power not only provided for the physical needs of his family and the nations, but it also symbolized the restoration of what had been lost. The relationships that had been broken by betrayal were healed, and the dreams that had once seemed impossible were fulfilled. In the same way, the resurrection of Christ is the fulfillment of God's promise to restore what has been broken by sin. It is the assurance that, just as Christ was raised from the dead, so too will we be raised to new life in Him.

The Role Of Suffering In The Reversal Of Fortune

One of the key elements of Joseph's story—and of the resurrection narrative—is the role that suffering plays in the reversal of fortune. Joseph's rise to power was preceded by years of suffering, betrayal, and hardship. Yet, it was through this suffering that God was at work, preparing Joseph for the role he would eventually play in saving his family and the nations. In the same way, Christ's exaltation was preceded by His suffering and death on the cross. In Isaiah 53:3, the prophet foretells of the Messiah, saying, "He was despised and rejected by mankind, a man of suffering, and familiar with pain."

Suffering, in both Joseph's story and in the life of Christ, is not meaningless—it is part of God's redemptive plan. Through suffering, God brings about the reversal of fortune, lifting the lowly and exalting the humble. Joseph's time in the pit and in prison was not wasted—it was the crucible through which his character was refined and his faith was strengthened. Similarly, Christ's suffering on the cross was not the end of the story—it was the means by which redemption was accomplished.

For believers, Joseph's story offers a powerful reminder that suffering is often the precursor to the reversal of fortune. Just as Joseph's life was redeemed and restored after years of hardship, so too are we promised that our suffering will one day give way to glory. In 2 Corinthians 4:17, Paul writes, "For our light and momentary troubles are achieving for us an eternal glory that far outweighs them all." The resurrection is the ultimate reversal of fortune—a promise that the suffering of this present life will one day give way to the eternal life and glory that is found in Christ.

The Reversal Of Fortune As A Foreshadowing Of Resurrection

As we reflect on Joseph's life and its prophetic connection to the resurrection of Christ, we see that Joseph's story is not just a tale of personal triumph—it is a powerful picture of God's redemptive plan. The reversal of fortune that Joseph experienced, from the pit to the palace, is a foreshadowing of the ultimate reversal of fortune found in the resurrection of Christ. Through His death and resurrection, Christ has defeated sin and death, offering new life to all who believe.

For believers, Joseph's story serves as a reminder that no matter how deep the pit, no matter how dark the prison, God's power to redeem and restore is greater. The resurrection is the ultimate act of God's sovereignty, the moment when death is defeated, and new life begins. Just as Joseph's life was redeemed and restored, so too are we promised that through Christ, we will be raised to new life and share in His eternal reign.

As we look forward to the final resurrection, we can take comfort in the knowledge that, just as God lifted Joseph from the pit and exalted him to a place of authority, He will one day lift us from the suffering and trials of this life and bring us into the fullness of His kingdom. The reversal of fortune that Joseph experienced is a prophetic picture of the hope of resurrection and new life for all who place their trust in Christ.

Chapter 18: Study Questions For Reflection

Preparation for Physical and Spiritual Provision:

1. How does Joseph's provision during the famine symbolize spiritual preparation?
2. In what ways can believers prepare for spiritual challenges like Joseph prepared for the famine?

CHAPTER 19: JOSEPH AS A TYPE OF THE SUFFERING SERVANT (ISAIAH 53)

Joseph's story, which unfolds across the latter half of the Book of Genesis, is a rich tapestry of suffering, redemption, and divine providence. At its heart, it is the story of a man who suffers unjustly, not for his own sake, but for the sake of others. Joseph's betrayal by his brothers, his descent into slavery and imprisonment, and his eventual rise to power in Egypt serve as more than just the dramatic highs and lows of a biblical hero—they point to a deeper theological truth, one that finds its fullest expression in Isaiah's prophecy of the Suffering Servant.

In Isaiah 53, the prophet describes a figure who is "despised and rejected by men, a man of sorrows, and familiar with suffering" (Isaiah 53:3). This Servant, though innocent, bears the iniquities of others and suffers on their behalf, ultimately bringing about their healing and redemption. The connections between this prophetic Servant and the life of Joseph are striking. Joseph's suffering, like that of the Suffering Servant, is not random or meaningless—it is part of God's redemptive plan. Through Joseph's suffering, not only his family but also the nations of the world are saved from death and famine. In this way, Joseph becomes a living foreshadowing of the ultimate Suffering Servant, Christ, whose atoning sacrifice would bring salvation to the entire world.

As we delve deeper into this connection, we will explore how Joseph's suffering mirrors the Suffering Servant's innocent suffering, how his endurance through trials reflects the endurance of the Messiah, and how the redemption brought through Joseph points forward to the greater redemption brought through Christ.

Joseph's Innocent Suffering: A Reflection Of The Servant's Affliction

Joseph's suffering begins with an act of betrayal, one of the most painful and unjust experiences a person can endure. His brothers, motivated by jealousy and hatred, conspire against him, casting him into a pit and then selling him into slavery. This act of betrayal is not unlike the rejection that the Suffering Servant faces in Isaiah 53. Isaiah writes, "He was despised and rejected by men" (Isaiah 53:3), a description that fits Joseph's experience. Though Joseph had done nothing to deserve his brothers' hatred, he becomes the object of their scorn, cast aside and sold into a life of bondage.

Joseph's innocence in the face of such harsh treatment mirrors the innocence of the Suffering Servant. Isaiah emphasizes that the Servant "had done no violence, nor was any deceit in his mouth" (Isaiah 53:9), yet he is "pierced for our transgressions" and "crushed for our iniquities" (Isaiah 53:5). The Suffering Servant bears the consequences of sins he did not commit, just as Joseph bears the consequences of his brothers' jealousy and treachery. Both Joseph and the Servant endure suffering not because of their own actions, but because of the sins and wrongdoings of others.

What is particularly significant about Joseph's suffering is that, despite the injustice of it, he does not allow bitterness or hatred to take root in his heart. This mirrors the character of the Suffering Servant, who, though he suffers grievously, "did not open his mouth; he was led like a lamb to the slaughter" (Isaiah 53:7). Joseph, like the Servant, remains silent in the face of injustice. His trust in God's providence allows him to endure suffering without losing his integrity or faith. This patient endurance is a key characteristic of both Joseph and the Suffering Servant, showing us a model of how to suffer righteously and with trust in God's greater plan.

Endurance Through Trials: The Servant And Joseph's Shared Path Of Suffering

The suffering of the Suffering Servant in Isaiah 53 is not limited to physical pain—it is a holistic affliction, one that touches every aspect of life. The Servant is "a man of sorrows, and familiar with suffering" (Isaiah 53:3), indicating that his suffering is continual and pervasive. Similarly, Joseph's trials are not confined to a single event; they span years of his life, from his betrayal and enslavement to his unjust imprisonment in Egypt. Joseph endures these trials without seeing an immediate end or purpose, yet he trusts in the providence of God.

Joseph's time in prison, after being falsely accused by Potiphar's wife, stands as a particularly poignant example of his endurance in the face of undeserved suffering. Like the Suffering Servant, Joseph suffers for crimes he did not commit. His imprisonment is a period of testing and refining, much like the trials the Servant undergoes. It is in this place of suffering that Joseph's character is most fully formed. Though he is forgotten by the very people he helped—much like the Servant, who is "despised and rejected" (Isaiah 53:3)—Joseph continues to trust in God's plan.

The endurance of both Joseph and the Servant reveals a

profound theological truth: suffering is not wasted in God's economy. In both stories, suffering becomes the pathway to redemption. Isaiah tells us that "by his wounds we are healed" (Isaiah 53:5), a statement that captures the paradox of redemptive suffering. Just as the Servant's suffering brings healing to others, Joseph's suffering ultimately leads to the preservation of life. Through his suffering, Joseph is positioned to save not only his family but also the surrounding nations from famine. His endurance is not merely for his own sake, but for the sake of others.

In this way, Joseph becomes a type of the Suffering Servant, demonstrating that suffering, when borne righteously, can become a channel through which God brings about His redemptive purposes. The suffering of the righteous, far from being meaningless, is often the means by which God's salvation is accomplished.

Redemption Through Suffering: Joseph's Role As A Savior Of Nations

Joseph's role as a savior through his suffering is perhaps the most striking parallel to the Suffering Servant. After enduring years of hardship, Joseph is elevated to a position of power in Egypt, where he is entrusted with the task of preparing for the coming famine. This elevation is not just a personal vindication —it is the fulfillment of God's plan to save lives. Joseph's wisdom and leadership during the famine result in the survival of many, including his own family.

In this way, Joseph's suffering leads to the salvation of the nations, just as the Suffering Servant's affliction leads to the salvation of humanity. Isaiah writes, "He bore the sin of many, and made intercession for the transgressors" (Isaiah 53:12). The Servant's suffering is not for himself, but for the benefit of others. Through his wounds, many are healed. Joseph's suffering serves a similar purpose: through his unjust affliction, he is placed in a position to save countless lives during the famine.

It is important to note that Joseph's role as a savior is not limited to the physical realm. His reconciliation with his brothers points to a deeper spiritual truth—one of forgiveness and restoration. When Joseph reveals himself to his brothers, he does not seek revenge for their betrayal. Instead, he offers forgiveness, saying, "You intended to harm me, but God intended it for good to accomplish what is now being done, the saving of many lives" (Genesis 50:20). This act of forgiveness echoes the work of the Suffering Servant, who "bore the sin of many" and through whose suffering we are forgiven and reconciled to God.

Joseph's role as a savior of nations and his act of forgiveness both point to the ultimate fulfillment of this pattern in Christ. Just as Joseph's suffering brought physical salvation to Egypt and Israel, Christ's suffering brings spiritual salvation to all who believe. And just as Joseph's forgiveness restored his relationship with his brothers, Christ's atoning sacrifice restores our relationship with God, reconciling us to the Father.

The Atoning Work Of Christ: Fulfillment Of The Suffering Servant Prophecy

While Joseph's life provides a powerful foreshadowing of the Suffering Servant, it is in Christ that the prophecy of Isaiah 53 is fully realized. Christ's suffering on the cross is the ultimate act of innocent suffering for the sake of others. Like Joseph, Christ was betrayed by those closest to him—his own disciple, Judas, handed him over to be crucified. Like Joseph, Christ was falsely accused and suffered for crimes he did not commit. But whereas Joseph's suffering resulted in the saving of physical lives, Christ's suffering results in the eternal salvation of souls.

Isaiah 53 describes the Servant as one who "was pierced for our transgressions, he was crushed for our iniquities; the punishment that brought us peace was on him, and by his wounds we are healed" (Isaiah 53:5). This passage captures the essence of Christ's atoning work on the cross. Through his suffering and death, Christ bore the sins of the world, offering himself as the ultimate sacrifice. His wounds bring healing not just for a season, as Joseph's leadership during the famine did, but for eternity.

In this way, Joseph's life points forward to the greater reality of Christ's atoning sacrifice. The parallels between Joseph and the Suffering Servant are not coincidental—they are part of God's divine plan to reveal the nature of His redemptive work. Joseph's story gives us a glimpse of the suffering, endurance, and ultimate redemption that would be fully accomplished in Christ.

Joseph As A Prefiguration Of The Suffering Servant

As we reflect on the life of Joseph and its connection to the prophecy of the Suffering Servant in Isaiah 53, we see that Joseph's story is more than just a narrative of personal endurance and triumph—it is a prophetic picture of the redemptive suffering that would be fully realized in Christ. Joseph's innocent suffering, his endurance through trials, and his role as a savior of nations all point to the work of the Suffering Servant, who would suffer not for his own sake, but for the sake of others.

In Christ, the prophecy of Isaiah 53 finds its ultimate fulfillment. Through his atoning sacrifice, Christ brings about the healing and reconciliation that Joseph's life foreshadowed. The parallels between Joseph and the Suffering Servant remind us that suffering, when borne righteously, has the power to bring about redemption. Just as Joseph's suffering saved lives, so too does Christ's suffering offer salvation to all who believe.

Joseph's life, then, stands as a testament to the profound

truth that God's redemptive plan often involves suffering—but that suffering is never the end of the story. Through suffering comes redemption, through endurance comes reconciliation, and through Christ's wounds, we are healed.

Chapter 19: Study Questions For Reflection

The Prophetic Nature of Joseph's Life:

1. How does Joseph's life serve as a prophetic type of Christ's role as Savior?
2. What lessons can we draw from the parallels between Joseph's life and biblical prophecy?

CHAPTER 20: JOSEPH'S FORGIVENESS AND RESTORATION AS A TYPE OF THE NEW COVENANT

Forgiveness, in its purest form, is not merely the absence of retribution; it is the restoration of relationship, the healing of deep wounds, and the offering of grace where none is deserved. In the story of Joseph, we witness a profound act of forgiveness that foreshadows the ultimate forgiveness offered through Christ under the New Covenant. Joseph's reunion with his brothers—those who sold him into slavery, betrayed his trust, and abandoned him to what they assumed would be certain death—is not marked by anger or vengeance. Instead, Joseph, standing in a position of unparalleled power, chooses to forgive and restore his family. This act of grace, seen in the reconciliation of Joseph and his brothers, serves as a type of the New Covenant, a foreshadowing of the forgiveness, renewal, and restoration that God offers to humanity through the sacrificial death of Christ.

In this chapter, we will explore how Joseph's forgiveness reflects the heart of the New Covenant as prophesied in Jeremiah 31:31-34. The New Covenant promises the transformation of the heart, the renewal of relationship, and the ultimate forgiveness of sin—a forgiveness that, like Joseph's, is undeserved and unconditional. Joseph's role as a model of forgiveness and reconciliation points forward to the greater work of Christ, whose death ushers in a new era of grace, healing the broken relationship between God and humanity.

The New Covenant: A Promise Of Forgiveness And Restoration

In the prophecy of Jeremiah 31:31-34, God promises a New Covenant with the house of Israel and the house of Judah, one that will be unlike the covenant made with their ancestors. The defining characteristic of this New Covenant is not merely external obedience to the law, but an internal transformation of the heart. "I will put my law in their minds and write it on their hearts. I will be their God, and they will be my people" (Jeremiah 31:33). This covenant, in contrast to the Old Covenant based on the Law, is marked by a deep, personal relationship between God and His people—one rooted in forgiveness and renewal. The New Covenant is God's promise to forgive the sins of His people and to restore the broken relationship between Himself and humanity.

This promise of forgiveness is central to the New Covenant: "For I will forgive their wickedness and will remember their sins no more" (Jeremiah 31:34). Under the Old Covenant, sin was dealt with through the sacrificial system, but the New Covenant offers a more profound form of forgiveness—one that removes sin completely, restoring humanity to a right relationship with God. This act of divine forgiveness finds its ultimate fulfillment in the sacrificial death of Christ, whose blood establishes the New Covenant and brings about the complete forgiveness of sins.

As we examine Joseph's act of forgiveness in light of the New Covenant, we begin to see how his actions prefigure the grace and restoration that God offers through Christ. Just as God, through Christ, offers unconditional forgiveness and restores His people to Himself, so too does Joseph offer forgiveness to his brothers, restoring the broken relationships within his family.

Joseph's Forgiveness: A Foreshadowing Of Divine Grace

The moment of Joseph's forgiveness comes after years of separation and suffering. His brothers, unaware of Joseph's true identity, come to Egypt seeking food during a time of famine. They do not recognize the man standing before them as their long-lost brother—the very one they betrayed and sold into slavery. Joseph, however, recognizes them immediately. Rather than seeking revenge, Joseph devises a plan to test their hearts, to see if they have changed since the day they betrayed him.

This testing period, during which Joseph hides his identity and puts his brothers through various trials, serves as a prelude to the act of forgiveness that will follow. When Joseph finally reveals himself to his brothers, the moment is filled with emotion. Genesis 45:3 describes the scene: "Joseph said to his brothers, 'I am Joseph! Is my father still living?' But his brothers were not able to answer him, because they were terrified at his presence." In this moment, the brothers are confronted with the full weight of their past sins. They are terrified, expecting Joseph to seek retribution for their betrayal.

But Joseph's response is one of grace, not vengeance. In Genesis 45:5, he tells them, "And now, do not be distressed and do not be angry with yourselves for selling me here, because it was to save lives that God sent me ahead of you." Joseph's ability to see God's hand at work in his suffering allows him to extend forgiveness to his brothers, despite the great wrong they had done to him. Rather than harboring bitterness, Joseph chooses to see his suffering as part of God's plan to preserve life. In this way, Joseph's forgiveness becomes a reflection of divine grace —a grace that sees beyond the sin and betrayal to the greater purpose of redemption.

Joseph's forgiveness is also marked by restoration. He not only forgives his brothers for their betrayal but also restores them to a place of honor within the family. He invites them to live in Egypt, to be near him, and to benefit from the abundance that he has been entrusted to oversee. This act of restoration mirrors the promise of the New Covenant, in which God not only forgives the sins of His people but also restores them to a right relationship with Himself. Just as Joseph's forgiveness leads to the healing of his family, the forgiveness offered under the New Covenant leads to the healing of the broken relationship between God and humanity.

Forgiveness And The Transformation Of The Heart: A New Covenant Reality

One of the central promises of the New Covenant is the transformation of the heart. In Jeremiah 31:33, God declares, "I will put my law in their minds and write it on their hearts." This internal transformation is what distinguishes the New Covenant from the Old. Under the Old Covenant, the law was external, written on stone tablets, and required strict obedience. But under the New Covenant, the law is written on the heart, transforming the individual from the inside out. This transformation leads to a new kind of relationship with God, one that is characterized by love, grace, and forgiveness.

Joseph's story offers a glimpse of this kind of transformation. When we first meet Joseph's brothers in Genesis, they are men consumed by jealousy, hatred, and self-interest. Their decision to sell Joseph into slavery is motivated by their envy of his favored status within the family. But by the time they encounter Joseph again in Egypt, their hearts have been changed. The testing that Joseph puts them through reveals this transformation. They no longer act out of selfishness; instead, they are willing to sacrifice for one another. Judah, in particular, offers to take Benjamin's place as a slave in Egypt, demonstrating a heart of humility and repentance (Genesis 44:33).

This transformation of Joseph's brothers foreshadows the transformation that takes place under the New Covenant. Just as the New Covenant promises a change of heart, Joseph's story illustrates how God can work in the lives of individuals to bring about true repentance and renewal. The brothers, once consumed by sin, are now ready to be restored to right relationship—both with Joseph and with God. This transformation is a necessary prelude to the forgiveness that Joseph offers, just as the transformation of the heart is a necessary part of the forgiveness offered under the New Covenant.

In this way, Joseph's forgiveness points to the deeper reality of the New Covenant: that true forgiveness and restoration are not merely external acts, but are rooted in the transformation of the heart. God's forgiveness under the New Covenant is not just a legal transaction—it is the beginning of a new relationship, one in which the heart is renewed and the individual is restored to full communion with God.

Joseph's Forgiveness And The Fulfillment Of The New Covenant In Christ

While Joseph's forgiveness offers a powerful foreshadowing of the New Covenant, it is in Christ that the promise of the New Covenant is fully realized. Jeremiah 31:34 speaks of a time when God will "forgive their wickedness and will remember their sins no more." This promise finds its ultimate fulfillment in the death and resurrection of Christ, whose atoning sacrifice establishes the New Covenant and brings about the forgiveness of sins for all who believe.

Just as Joseph forgave his brothers and restored them to relationship, Christ offers forgiveness to all who come to Him in faith. But whereas Joseph's forgiveness was limited to the temporal and familial realm, Christ's forgiveness extends to the eternal and spiritual realm. Through His death on the cross, Christ bears the weight of humanity's sin, offering a forgiveness that is complete and final. As the writer of Hebrews explains, "For this reason Christ is the mediator of a new covenant, that those who are called may receive the promised eternal inheritance—now that he has died as a ransom to set them free from the sins committed under the first covenant" (Hebrews 9:15).

Christ's forgiveness, like Joseph's, is not just about wiping the slate clean—it is about restoring a broken relationship. Through His sacrifice, Christ reconciles humanity to God, restoring the relationship that was broken by sin. This act of reconciliation is at the heart of the New Covenant. Paul writes in 2 Corinthians 5:18, "All this is from God, who reconciled us to himself through Christ and gave us the ministry of reconciliation." Just as Joseph's forgiveness led to the reconciliation of his family, Christ's forgiveness leads to the reconciliation of humanity with God.

Moreover, Christ's forgiveness is accompanied by the gift of the Holy Spirit, who enables the transformation of the heart promised in the New Covenant. Through the indwelling of the Spirit, believers are empowered to live in accordance with God's will, with His law written on their hearts. This transformation is what allows believers to experience the fullness of the forgiveness and restoration that the New Covenant offers.

Joseph's Forgiveness As A Reflection Of The New Covenant's Grace

Joseph's forgiveness of his brothers is one of the most profound moments in the biblical narrative, a moment that not only restores a family but also points to the greater restoration that God would accomplish through Christ. Joseph's willingness to forgive, to offer grace where none was deserved, and to restore his brothers to relationship serves as a powerful type of the New Covenant—a covenant marked by forgiveness, renewal, and restoration.

In Christ, the promises of the New Covenant are fully realized. Through His sacrificial death, Christ offers the complete and final forgiveness of sins, reconciling humanity to God and restoring the broken relationship that sin had severed. Like Joseph, Christ extends forgiveness not as a transaction but as an act of grace, one that transforms the heart and brings about true reconciliation.

As we reflect on Joseph's story in light of the New Covenant, we are reminded of the depth of God's grace, a grace that forgives, heals, and restores. Just as Joseph's forgiveness brought healing to his family, Christ's forgiveness brings healing to all who come to Him in faith, offering a new relationship with God, one that is marked by love, grace, and the promise of eternal life.

Chapter 20: Study Questions For Reflection

Trusting God's Sovereign Plan:

1. How does Joseph's life demonstrate trust in God's sovereignty?
2. How can we apply trust in God's sovereignty in our own lives?

CHAPTER 21: JOSEPH'S ROLE IN PRESERVING THE LINEAGE OF ISRAEL

Typology of Preservation for the Messiah

Joseph's rise to power in Egypt, while often understood as a personal triumph of faith, wisdom, and perseverance, also carries profound implications for the future of God's redemptive plan. By providing refuge and sustenance for his family during the years of famine, Joseph preserves not only the lives of his brothers and father but also the very lineage from which the Messiah would one day emerge. This act of preservation is not merely a family reunion; it is a pivotal moment in the unfolding of God's covenant promises to Abraham, Isaac, and Jacob. Through Joseph's leadership, the family of Israel is kept alive, safeguarded from the ravages of famine, and given the opportunity to grow into the great nation that God had promised.

In this chapter, we will explore how Joseph's role in preserving the family of Israel serves as a typological foreshadowing of God's preservation of the Davidic line for the birth of the Messiah. Just as Joseph's actions ensured the survival of his family, God's providential care throughout history ensured that the line of David—despite numerous threats—would remain intact until the coming of Christ. This theme of preservation speaks to God's faithfulness in fulfilling His promises, regardless of external circumstances, and highlights the lengths to which God will go to bring about the fulfillment of His redemptive plan.

Preserving The Line Of Jacob: Joseph's Providential Role In Salvation History

The famine that strikes the ancient world during Joseph's time is not a mere backdrop to his personal story—it is a critical event in salvation history. The famine threatens the very existence of Jacob's family, the small but chosen people through whom God had promised to bring blessing to the world. As the famine intensifies, Jacob and his sons find themselves on the brink of destruction, with no resources left in Canaan to sustain them. In a moment of desperation, they turn to Egypt, unaware that their brother Joseph, whom they betrayed and sold into slavery years earlier, now holds the power to save them.

Joseph's role in this moment is nothing short of providential. His ability to interpret Pharaoh's dreams and his wisdom in storing grain during the years of abundance allow Egypt to become the only place of refuge during the famine. When his brothers arrive in Egypt seeking food, Joseph recognizes them immediately, though they do not recognize him. This moment is not just a family reunion—it is the moment in which the future of God's covenant people is secured. Without Joseph's leadership and forgiveness, the family of Jacob would have perished in the famine, and the line of Israel would have been cut off.

The preservation of Jacob's family through Joseph is a direct fulfillment of God's promise to Abraham, Isaac, and Jacob that their descendants would become a great nation. In Genesis 12:2-3, God tells Abraham, "I will make you into a great nation, and I will bless you; I will make your name great, and you will be a blessing. I will bless those who bless you, and whoever curses you I will curse; and all peoples on earth will be blessed through you." This promise, which is passed down to Isaac and then to Jacob, hinges on the survival of their family. Without Joseph's intervention, the family of Israel would have been lost, and God's covenant promises would have appeared to be in jeopardy.

But as we see in Joseph's story, God's providential care ensures that His promises are never in jeopardy. Through Joseph's suffering, betrayal, and eventual rise to power, God weaves together a plan that not only saves Joseph's family but also ensures the continuation of the covenant line. This moment of preservation is a foreshadowing of the way God will continue to preserve His people throughout history, even in the face of seemingly insurmountable challenges.

The Lineage Of The Messiah: A Story Of Divine Preservation

The preservation of Jacob's family during the famine is not an isolated event in salvation history—it is part of a larger pattern of divine preservation that culminates in the birth of the Messiah. Throughout the history of Israel, we see repeated attempts to extinguish the covenant line, from threats of famine and war to internal strife and exile. And yet, time and again, God intervenes to preserve the family of Israel, ensuring that the line of David, from which the Messiah would come, remains intact.

The connection between Joseph's preservation of Jacob's family and the preservation of the Davidic line is profound. Just as Joseph's actions ensure the survival of the family of Israel, God's sovereign hand preserves the line of David, even when it seems that all hope is lost. In 2 Samuel 7:12-16, God makes a covenant with David, promising, "Your house and your kingdom will endure forever before me; your throne will be established forever." This promise, like the covenant made with Abraham, depends on the survival of David's lineage. And yet, throughout Israel's history, this lineage is threatened by external enemies, internal corruption, and the Babylonian exile.

Despite these challenges, God remains faithful to His covenant promises. Even during the exile, when it seemed that the Davidic line had been severed, God preserved a remnant of His people, ensuring that the line of David would continue. The genealogy of Jesus in Matthew 1 traces this line, demonstrating that, despite the many threats to Israel's survival, God's promise to David was fulfilled in the birth of Christ. The preservation of the Davidic line is a testament to God's faithfulness and His unwavering commitment to bringing about the salvation of the world through the Messiah.

Joseph's role in preserving the family of Israel during the famine foreshadows this divine preservation of the Messianic line. Just as Joseph's leadership and forgiveness ensured the survival of his brothers and the continuation of the covenant promises, God's providential care ensured that the line of David would remain intact until the coming of Christ. This theme of preservation, woven throughout both Joseph's story and the broader narrative of Israel's history, highlights the lengths to which God will go to fulfill His redemptive plan.

God's Faithfulness In Fulfilling His Promises

One of the most striking aspects of Joseph's story is the way it illustrates God's faithfulness in fulfilling His promises, even when circumstances seem to suggest otherwise. At multiple points in Joseph's life, it appears that God's promises are in jeopardy. When Joseph is sold into slavery by his brothers, it seems that the dream he had of ruling over his family will never come to pass. When he is falsely accused and imprisoned, it appears that his suffering has no purpose. And yet, through it all, God is at work, using even the most painful and unjust circumstances to bring about His plan.

This theme of God's faithfulness in the face of adversity is not limited to Joseph's life—it is a recurring theme throughout Scripture. In the New Testament, Paul writes in Romans 8:28, "And we know that in all things God works for the good of those who love him, who have been called according to his purpose." This truth is evident in Joseph's story, where God uses the evil intentions of his brothers and the unjust actions of Potiphar's wife to bring about the preservation of the covenant people. What appears to be a series of tragedies is, in fact, part of God's larger plan to fulfill His promises.

The preservation of Jacob's family through Joseph serves as a powerful reminder that God's promises are never in jeopardy. Even when circumstances seem dire, God is at work behind the scenes, ensuring that His covenant will be fulfilled. This is particularly evident in the way God preserves the line of Israel, ensuring that the family through whom the Messiah would come is kept alive during the famine. Just as Joseph's brothers could not have foreseen the way God would use their betrayal for good, the people of Israel could not have imagined the ways in which God would preserve the Davidic line through exile, war, and internal strife.

This faithfulness extends to the New Testament, where we see the ultimate fulfillment of God's promises in the birth, death, and resurrection of Jesus Christ. The preservation of the Davidic line, despite countless threats, leads directly to the coming of the Messiah, through whom God's redemptive plan for the world is realized. In Christ, we see the culmination of God's faithfulness, as He brings about the salvation of His people through the very line that Joseph helped to preserve.

Joseph's Role As A Foreshadowing Of The

Messiah's Work

In addition to preserving the physical lives of his family, Joseph's role as a protector and provider foreshadows the work of the Messiah, who would come to preserve and protect the spiritual lives of God's people. Just as Joseph provides food and refuge for his family during the famine, Jesus provides spiritual nourishment and refuge for those who come to Him in faith. In John 6:35, Jesus declares, "I am the bread of life. Whoever comes to me will never go hungry, and whoever believes in me will never be thirsty." Joseph's role in sustaining his family through physical famine points forward to Christ's role in sustaining His people through spiritual famine.

Furthermore, Joseph's forgiveness of his brothers and his willingness to restore them to relationship foreshadows Christ's work of reconciliation. Just as Joseph forgives his brothers and restores them to a place of honor within the family, Christ offers forgiveness and reconciliation to all who come to Him in faith. In 2 Corinthians 5:18-19, Paul writes, "All this is from God, who reconciled us to himself through Christ and gave us the ministry of reconciliation: that God was reconciling the world to himself in Christ, not counting people's sins against them." Joseph's role as a reconciler points to the greater work of reconciliation that Christ accomplishes through His death and resurrection.

In this way, Joseph's preservation of the family of Israel serves as a type of the Messiah's work of preserving and sustaining His people. Just as Joseph's actions ensured the survival of the covenant line, Christ's sacrificial death and resurrection ensure the spiritual survival of all who place their trust in Him. The preservation of the line of Israel, from which the Messiah would come, points forward to the greater preservation that Christ offers to His people, as He sustains them through trials and leads them into eternal life.

God's Providential Preservation And The Coming

Of The Messiah

Joseph's role in preserving the family of Israel during the famine is a pivotal moment in the history of God's covenant people. By providing refuge for his family in Egypt, Joseph not only saves their physical lives but also preserves the very lineage from which the Messiah would come. This theme of preservation is woven throughout the history of Israel, as God continues to safeguard the Davidic line, ensuring that His promises are fulfilled in the birth of Christ.

As we reflect on Joseph's story in light of the Messianic line, we are reminded of God's faithfulness in preserving His people, even in the face of seemingly insurmountable challenges. Joseph's actions foreshadow the work of Christ, who provides spiritual nourishment, protection, and reconciliation for all who come to Him in faith. Just as God preserved the family of Israel through Joseph, so too does He preserve His covenant promises through Christ, ensuring that His plan for the redemption of the world is brought to fruition.

In Joseph's story, we see a powerful testament to the lengths to which God will go to preserve His people and fulfill His promises. And in Christ, we see the ultimate fulfillment of those promises, as God's redemptive plan is realized through the preservation of the Messianic line and the salvation of all who believe.

Chapter 21: Study Questions For Reflection

Reflecting on Redemption and Restoration:
1. What role does redemption play in Joseph's story?
2. How does the theme of restoration in Joseph's story relate to God's ultimate plan for humanity?

CHAPTER 22: JOSEPH AS A TYPE OF INTERCESSOR

In the grand narrative of Joseph's life, we find more than a story of personal redemption and leadership. Joseph's unique position between Pharaoh and the people of Egypt, as well as between his family and Pharaoh, offers us a striking image of mediation and intercession. His role as a mediator in times of crisis serves as a powerful foreshadowing of Christ's priestly role as the ultimate intercessor, standing between humanity and God. Just as Joseph mediated on behalf of those who could not speak for themselves, Christ continually intercedes for us before the Father, ensuring that we receive mercy and grace in our time of need.

In Hebrews 7:25, we read, "Therefore he is able to save completely those who come to God through him, because he always lives to intercede for them." This verse highlights Christ's ongoing role as our intercessor, continually standing in the gap between a holy God and sinful humanity. In Joseph's life, we see glimpses of this priestly role as he intercedes for the people of Egypt, negotiating their survival during the famine, and as he mediates for his family, securing their safety and provision in a foreign land. Joseph's ability to stand between two worlds

—his Hebrew heritage and his Egyptian authority—gives us a prophetic glimpse of Christ, who bridges the gap between heaven and earth, between God and humanity.

As we explore Joseph's role as an intercessor, we will see how his actions reflect Christ's work of mediation and intercession. We will examine how Joseph's position of authority enabled him to intercede on behalf of those in need and how his willingness to advocate for his family mirrors Christ's ongoing advocacy for believers before the Father.

Joseph's Mediation For The People Of Egypt: A Type Of Christ's Intercession For Humanity

One of the most striking aspects of Joseph's role in Egypt is his position as a mediator between Pharaoh and the people during the famine. After interpreting Pharaoh's dreams and predicting the coming years of abundance followed by years of famine, Joseph is entrusted with the task of managing Egypt's resources. In Genesis 41:40, Pharaoh declares, "You shall be in charge of my palace, and all my people are to submit to your orders. Only with respect to the throne will I be greater than you." With this authority, Joseph becomes the intermediary between Pharaoh's power and the needs of the people.

As the famine spreads and the people of Egypt begin to suffer, they turn to Joseph for help. In Genesis 41:55, we read, "When all Egypt began to feel the famine, the people cried to Pharaoh for food. Then Pharaoh told all the Egyptians, 'Go to Joseph and do what he tells you.'" Joseph's role here is not simply administrative; he becomes the one to whom the people turn in their time of need, the one who mediates between their desperation and Pharaoh's authority. Joseph distributes the stored grain, ensuring that the people are sustained through the years of famine.

This role of mediator and provider points to Christ's work

of intercession for humanity. Just as Joseph stood between Pharaoh's power and the people's needs, Christ stands between God's holiness and humanity's brokenness. In 1 Timothy 2:5, Paul writes, "For there is one God and one mediator between God and mankind, the man Christ Jesus." Like Joseph, Christ is the one to whom we turn in times of spiritual famine, the one who intercedes on our behalf and provides us with the sustenance we need—grace, mercy, and eternal life.

Joseph's actions during the famine also reflect Christ's role as the bread of life. In John 6:35, Jesus declares, "I am the bread of life. Whoever comes to me will never go hungry, and whoever believes in me will never be thirsty." Just as Joseph provided physical bread to sustain the people of Egypt during the famine, Christ provides spiritual bread to sustain us in our spiritual hunger. Joseph's mediation in Egypt becomes a prophetic image of Christ's greater work of intercession, providing not only for our physical needs but for our deepest spiritual needs as well.

Joseph's Intercession For His Family: A Foreshadowing Of Christ's Advocacy For Believers

In addition to mediating for the people of Egypt, Joseph also intercedes for his own family, securing their safety and provision during the famine. When Joseph's brothers come to Egypt seeking food, they do not recognize him, but Joseph immediately recognizes them. Despite their betrayal years earlier, Joseph does not respond with anger or retribution. Instead, he tests their hearts, seeking to discern whether they have changed. After several interactions, Joseph finally reveals his identity to his brothers in a moment of profound grace and forgiveness.

In Genesis 45:4-5, Joseph says to his brothers, "I am your brother Joseph, the one you sold into Egypt! And now, do not be distressed and do not be angry with yourselves for selling me here, because it was to save lives that God sent me ahead of you." Joseph's forgiveness of his brothers is itself an act of intercession —he stands between their guilt and the consequences they deserve, offering them grace instead of punishment. But Joseph's intercession does not end with forgiveness. He goes further, securing their safety and provision by inviting them to live in Egypt under his protection.

Joseph's intercession for his family mirrors Christ's role as our advocate before the Father. In 1 John 2:1, we read, "But if anybody does sin, we have an advocate with the Father—Jesus Christ, the Righteous One." Just as Joseph interceded on behalf of his brothers, forgiving their sins and providing for their future, Christ intercedes on our behalf, advocating for us before the Father and securing our eternal future. Christ's advocacy is not just a one-time event; it is an ongoing work of intercession, as Hebrews 7:25 reminds us: "Therefore he is able to save completely those who come to God through him, because he always lives to intercede for them."

Joseph's willingness to forgive his brothers and restore them to a place of honor within the family points forward to the way Christ intercedes for believers, securing our place in the family of God. Through His death and resurrection, Christ not only forgives our sins but also restores us to right relationship with the Father, securing our adoption as sons and daughters of God. Just as Joseph's intercession brought healing and restoration to his family, Christ's intercession brings healing and restoration to our relationship with God.

The Priesthood Of Christ: Joseph's Mediation As A Foreshadowing Of Christ's Priestly Role

Joseph's role as an intercessor also points to the larger biblical theme of priesthood. In the Old Testament, the priests served as mediators between God and the people, offering sacrifices on behalf of the people and interceding for them before God. In this way, the priesthood served as a foreshadowing of Christ's ultimate role as the Great High Priest, the one who would offer Himself as the final and perfect sacrifice and who would continually intercede for His people before the Father.

Joseph's mediation between Pharaoh and the people, and between his family and Pharaoh, reflects this priestly function. Although Joseph is not a priest in the formal sense, his actions carry the weight of mediation and intercession. He acts as a bridge between two parties—Pharaoh and the people of Egypt, Pharaoh and his family—and through his intercession, he ensures that both are provided for. This role of intercessor points forward to Christ, who not only acts as our mediator but also fulfills the role of High Priest, offering Himself as the perfect sacrifice for sin and continually interceding for us before the Father.

In Hebrews 4:14-16, we read, "Therefore, since we have a great high priest who has ascended into heaven, Jesus the Son of God, let us hold firmly to the faith we profess. For we do not have a high priest who is unable to empathize with our weaknesses, but we have one who has been tempted in every way, just as we are —yet he did not sin. Let us then approach God's throne of grace with confidence, so that we may receive mercy and find grace to help us in our time of need." Christ's role as High Priest is one of intercession and empathy—He understands our weaknesses and continually intercedes for us, offering us mercy and grace in our time of need.

Joseph's mediation during the famine foreshadows this priestly role of Christ. Just as Joseph stood in the gap between Pharaoh's power and the people's need, Christ stands in the gap between God's holiness and our brokenness, offering Himself as the ultimate mediator and High Priest. Through His sacrifice and ongoing intercession, Christ ensures that we have access to the Father and that we receive the mercy and grace we need.

The Ongoing Work Of Intercession: Christ As The Eternal Mediator

One of the most significant aspects of Christ's intercession is its ongoing nature. Unlike the priests of the Old Testament, who had to offer sacrifices repeatedly, Christ's sacrifice was once for all, and His intercession is eternal. Hebrews 7:27 says, "He sacrificed for their sins once for all when he offered himself." This once-for-all sacrifice is the foundation of Christ's eternal intercession. Because His sacrifice was perfect and complete, His intercession never ceases. He continually advocates for us before the Father, ensuring that we are covered by His grace and righteousness.

Joseph's role as a mediator during the famine points to this ongoing work of intercession. Throughout the years of famine, Joseph did not just provide a one-time solution; he continually mediated between Pharaoh and the people, ensuring that their needs were met for the duration of the crisis. In the same way, Christ's intercession is not a one-time event but an ongoing work. He continually intercedes for us, advocating for us before the Father and ensuring that we are covered by His grace.

This ongoing intercession is a source of great comfort for believers. It means that no matter how often we fail or fall short, Christ is always there, standing in the gap for us, advocating for us before the Father. Just as Joseph's mediation ensured the survival of Egypt during the famine, Christ's intercession ensures our spiritual survival, providing us with the grace and mercy we need to navigate the trials of life.

Joseph As A Type Of Christ's Intercessory Role

As we reflect on Joseph's role as an intercessor, we see a powerful foreshadowing of Christ's priestly work. Joseph's mediation between Pharaoh and the people of Egypt, and between his family and Pharaoh, points to Christ's ultimate role as the mediator between God and humanity. Just as Joseph provided for the physical needs of Egypt and his family during the famine, Christ provides for our deepest spiritual needs through His ongoing intercession.

Joseph's willingness to stand in the gap for those in need, to forgive his brothers, and to secure their future, mirrors Christ's ongoing work of advocacy for believers. Through His death and resurrection, Christ not only reconciles us to the Father but also continues to intercede for us, ensuring that we receive the grace and mercy we need to live in right relationship with God.

In Joseph's story, we see a glimpse of the greater work of Christ, who stands as the eternal mediator, continually interceding for us before the Father and securing our eternal salvation. Just as Joseph's intercession brought life and provision to those in need, Christ's intercession brings eternal life and spiritual provision to all who come to Him in faith.

Chapter 22: Study Questions For Reflection

Joseph's Legacy as a Model of Faith:
1. What aspects of Joseph's life form his legacy?
2. How can believers apply Joseph's legacy of faith to their lives today?

CHAPTER 23: THE TYPOLOGY OF DREAMS: REVELATION AND GOD'S PLAN

Dreams occupy a central place in the life of Joseph, both as markers of his destiny and as instruments of God's revelation to guide the unfolding of His plan. From the very beginning of Joseph's story, his dreams set him apart, igniting the jealousy of his brothers and propelling him on a journey of betrayal, suffering, and eventual redemption. Yet Joseph's dreams, and his ability to interpret the dreams of others, were not random occurrences; they were deliberate acts of divine communication, tools through which God revealed His will and shaped the course of history.

In Joseph's life, dreams serve as a vehicle for prophecy, offering glimpses into the future and revealing the purposes of God. Joseph's own dreams, which foretold his rise to prominence, and his interpretation of Pharaoh's dreams, which saved Egypt from famine, both point to the larger theme of God using visions and dreams to communicate His redemptive plan. This typological connection between Joseph's dreams and the broader biblical theme of divine revelation invites us to consider how God uses dreams and visions throughout Scripture to reveal His will—culminating in the apocalyptic visions of the Book of Revelation.

In this chapter, we will explore how Joseph's role as a receiver and interpreter of divine dreams foreshadows the greater work of revelation in Scripture. We will examine the typological connection between Joseph's dreams and the prophetic visions found throughout the Bible, particularly in the New Testament, where the ultimate revelation of God's redemptive plan is unveiled in Christ. Joseph's life offers us a glimpse of how God communicates His purposes through dreams, inviting us to trust in His sovereign plan even when it is only partially revealed.

Joseph's Early Dreams: The Seeds Of Destiny And The Prophetic Nature Of Divine Revelation

Joseph's story begins with a pair of dreams that set the stage for his entire life's trajectory. In Genesis 37:5-9, we read of Joseph's two dreams: in the first, he dreams of binding sheaves of grain in the field, and his sheaf rises and stands upright, while his brothers' sheaves gather around and bow down to his; in the second, he dreams that the sun, moon, and eleven stars bow down to him. These dreams, which Joseph shares with his brothers and father, ignite the jealousy and hatred that ultimately lead to his betrayal and sale into slavery.

At first glance, Joseph's dreams seem audacious, even arrogant. But these dreams are not the product of Joseph's imagination or youthful ambition—they are divine revelations, glimpses of the future that God has ordained for him. The dreams foretell Joseph's rise to power and his eventual role as the savior of his family, who will one day come to Egypt seeking his help during the famine. What is remarkable about these dreams is not only their accuracy but also the way they set in motion the events that will lead to their fulfillment.

In this sense, Joseph's dreams are prophetic in nature. They are not mere symbols or metaphors; they are divinely inspired revelations that reveal the future course of Joseph's life and the lives of those around him. This prophetic quality of Joseph's dreams places them within the broader biblical tradition of God using dreams and visions to communicate His will. Throughout Scripture, God reveals His plan to His people through dreams, from the visions given to Daniel and Ezekiel to the apocalyptic revelations of John in the Book of Revelation.

Joseph's early dreams serve as a typological precursor to these later biblical visions. Just as Joseph's dreams reveal his destiny and the future of his family, the prophetic visions in Scripture reveal the future course of God's redemptive plan for humanity. Joseph's dreams are a microcosm of the larger biblical pattern of revelation—where God unveils His plan piece by piece, inviting His people to trust in His sovereignty even when the full picture is not yet clear.

The Interpretation Of Pharaoh's Dreams: Joseph As The Mediator Of Divine Revelation

Joseph's ability to interpret dreams is not limited to his own visions. While in Egypt, Joseph is called upon to interpret the dreams of others, most notably Pharaoh's dreams, which serve as warnings of an impending famine. In Genesis 41, Pharaoh dreams of seven healthy cows being devoured by seven gaunt cows, and seven heads of grain, full and good, being consumed by seven thin and scorched heads of grain. Disturbed by these dreams and unable to find an interpreter among his advisors, Pharaoh turns to Joseph, who is known for his ability to interpret dreams with divine insight.

Joseph's interpretation of Pharaoh's dreams reveals a pattern of divine revelation: the dreams are not random or meaningless; they are warnings from God, offering Pharaoh the opportunity to prepare for the coming disaster. Joseph tells Pharaoh, "The dreams of Pharaoh are one and the same. God has revealed to Pharaoh what he is about to do" (Genesis 41:25). In this moment, Joseph becomes the mediator of divine revelation, standing between God and Pharaoh to deliver the message that will save Egypt and the surrounding nations from destruction.

Joseph's role as the interpreter of Pharaoh's dreams is significant for several reasons. First, it highlights the fact that dreams are one of the ways God communicates His will to humanity. Pharaoh's dreams are not the product of his own subconscious fears; they are divinely inspired visions, intended to reveal the future and guide Pharaoh's actions. Second, Joseph's ability to interpret the dreams points to his unique role as a mediator of revelation. Just as Joseph stands between Pharaoh and God to interpret the meaning of the dreams, so too do the prophets of Scripture stand between God and humanity, delivering His messages and revealing His will.

This typological connection between Joseph's role as an interpreter of dreams and the broader theme of prophecy in Scripture foreshadows the ultimate revelation of God's plan in Christ. Just as Joseph interprets Pharaoh's dreams to reveal God's will, Christ is the ultimate mediator of divine revelation, revealing the fullness of God's redemptive plan. In John 1:18, we read, "No one has ever seen God, but the one and only Son, who is himself God and is in closest relationship with the Father, has made him known." Christ is the one who reveals God to humanity, not just in part, but in full. Joseph's role as a mediator of divine revelation serves as a foreshadowing of Christ's ultimate role as the mediator between God and humanity, revealing the full scope of God's plan for salvation.

The Typology Of Dreams In Biblical Prophecy: Joseph And The Prophetic Tradition

Joseph's dreams, and his ability to interpret the dreams of others, place him within the broader biblical tradition of prophecy and revelation. Throughout Scripture, God uses dreams and visions to reveal His will to His people, offering glimpses of the future and guiding their actions. In the Old Testament, we see this pattern repeated in the lives of the prophets, who are often given visions that reveal God's plans for His people and for the world.

One of the most striking examples of this is the prophet Daniel, whose ability to interpret dreams parallels that of Joseph. Like Joseph, Daniel is called upon to interpret the dreams of a foreign ruler, King Nebuchadnezzar, and like Joseph, Daniel's interpretations reveal God's sovereign control over the future. In Daniel 2, Nebuchadnezzar dreams of a great statue made of various materials, which is ultimately destroyed by a rock "not cut by human hands." Daniel interprets the dream as a prophecy of the rise and fall of kingdoms, culminating in the establishment of God's eternal kingdom. This dream, like Pharaoh's dreams in Genesis, reveals God's control over history and His plan for the future.

The connection between Joseph and Daniel highlights the typological role of dreams in biblical prophecy. Both Joseph and Daniel serve as mediators of divine revelation, interpreting dreams that reveal God's will and guiding the actions of powerful rulers. Their ability to interpret dreams points to the larger theme of God using visions and prophecy to communicate His plan to His people. In this sense, Joseph's dreams are part of a larger typological pattern, one that culminates in the apocalyptic visions of the New Testament.

In the Book of Revelation, we see the ultimate expression of this typology. John's visions reveal the final stages of God's redemptive plan, offering a glimpse of the end times and the establishment of God's eternal kingdom. Just as Joseph's dreams reveal the future course of his life and the fate of his family, John's visions reveal the future course of history and the fate of all creation. In Revelation 1:1, we read, "The revelation from Jesus Christ, which God gave him to show his servants what must soon take place." This revelation, like Joseph's dreams, is a divine gift, offering a glimpse of God's plan for the future.

The typological connection between Joseph's dreams and the prophetic visions of Scripture invites us to consider how God reveals His will throughout history. Dreams, visions, and prophecy are not random or isolated events; they are part of a larger pattern of divine communication, through which God reveals His plan piece by piece. Joseph's role as a receiver and interpreter of dreams serves as a foreshadowing of the greater revelation that would come through Christ, the one who reveals the fullness of God's redemptive plan.

The Fulfillment Of God's Redemptive Plan In Christ: From Dreams To Revelation

While Joseph's dreams reveal the future course of his life and the fate of his family, they are ultimately part of a larger story—one that points forward to the fulfillment of God's redemptive plan in Christ. Joseph's dreams, like the dreams and visions throughout Scripture, are not ends in themselves; they are glimpses of a larger narrative, one that finds its ultimate fulfillment in the life, death, and resurrection of Jesus Christ.

In the New Testament, we see the culmination of God's plan, revealed not through dreams but through the person of Christ. In Hebrews 1:1-2, we read, "In the past God spoke to our ancestors through the prophets at many times and in various ways, but in these last days he has spoken to us by his Son, whom he appointed heir of all things, and through whom also he made the universe." Christ is the final and complete revelation of God's will, the one who brings to fulfillment the redemptive plan that had been revealed in part through dreams, visions, and prophecy.

Joseph's role as a receiver and interpreter of dreams points to this larger reality. His dreams are a foreshadowing of the ultimate revelation that would come through Christ, the one who not only reveals God's plan but also brings it to fulfillment. Just as Joseph's dreams set the course for his life and the salvation of his family, Christ's life and work set the course for the salvation of all humanity.

The typological connection between Joseph's dreams and the broader theme of divine revelation invites us to trust in God's plan, even when it is only partially revealed. Like Joseph, we may not always understand the full meaning of the dreams and visions we receive, but we can trust that God is at work, revealing His will and guiding our lives according to His sovereign plan. And just as Joseph's dreams were ultimately fulfilled, so too will God's redemptive plan be brought to completion through Christ, the one who reveals the fullness of God's will and brings it to pass.

Joseph's Dreams And The Unfolding Of God's Plan

As we reflect on the role of dreams in Joseph's life, we see a powerful typological connection to the broader theme of divine revelation in Scripture. Joseph's dreams, and his ability to interpret the dreams of others, serve as a prophetic precursor to the visions and prophecies that reveal God's plan throughout history. From the dreams of Pharaoh to the apocalyptic visions of John in Revelation, God uses dreams and visions to communicate His will and guide the course of history.

Joseph's role as a receiver and interpreter of dreams invites us to consider how God reveals His plan in our own lives. Like Joseph, we may not always understand the full meaning of the dreams and visions we receive, but we can trust that God is at work, revealing His will and guiding us according to His sovereign plan. And just as Joseph's dreams were ultimately fulfilled, so too will God's redemptive plan be brought to completion through Christ, the one who reveals the fullness of God's will and brings it to pass.

In Joseph's story, we see a powerful testament to the way God communicates His will through dreams and visions, offering us glimpses of His plan and inviting us to trust in His sovereign purpose. And in Christ, we see the ultimate fulfillment of that plan, as God's redemptive purposes are revealed and brought to completion in the one who is the true mediator of divine revelation.

Chapter 23: Study Questions For Reflection

Lessons in Humility and Obedience

1. What role does humility play in Joseph's journey?
2. How does obedience shape Joseph's relationship with God?

CHAPTER 24: JOSEPH AS A TYPE OF THE RIGHTEOUS SUFFERER (PSALM 22)

Suffering is an inescapable part of the human condition, but for the righteous sufferer, it carries a deeper, spiritual weight. Psalm 22, a psalm often regarded as prophetic of Christ's suffering on the cross, poignantly captures the experience of a person who feels abandoned by God yet continues to place their trust in Him for deliverance. The psalm begins with the haunting cry, "My God, my God, why have you forsaken me?" (Psalm 22:1), a cry echoed by Christ Himself during His crucifixion. Yet despite the profound anguish of this lament, the psalm ends with an expression of faith in God's ultimate deliverance and vindication.

Joseph's life, with its profound arc of suffering and redemption, offers a striking typological connection to the righteous sufferer described in Psalm 22. Like the figure in the psalm, Joseph is an innocent man who suffers unjustly. He is betrayed by his brothers, falsely accused by Potiphar's wife, and forgotten in prison. Through it all, Joseph remains faithful to God, trusting in His sovereignty even when deliverance seems distant. Joseph's endurance through suffering, marked by both faith and patience, prefigures the ultimate righteous sufferer—Christ—who endures the cross with unwavering trust in God's redemptive plan.

In this chapter, we will explore how Joseph's experience of suffering serves as a type of the righteous sufferer, pointing forward to Christ's own endurance on the cross. By examining the parallels between Joseph's trials and the themes of Psalm 22, we gain deeper insight into the nature of righteous suffering, the role of faith in the midst of affliction, and the ultimate promise of deliverance for those who trust in God.

Joseph's Betrayal And Imprisonment: The Beginning Of The Righteous Sufferer's Journey

Joseph's journey as a righteous sufferer begins with betrayal. In Genesis 37, Joseph's brothers, fueled by jealousy over their father's favoritism and Joseph's prophetic dreams, plot to kill him. Instead, they decide to sell him into slavery, casting him into a pit before selling him to passing traders. This act of betrayal marks the first in a series of profound injustices that Joseph will endure. He is torn from his family, stripped of his favored status, and sent to a foreign land where he will live as a slave.

This moment of betrayal parallels the opening cry of Psalm 22: "My God, my God, why have you forsaken me?" (Psalm 22:1). Joseph, though not recorded as uttering these words, surely felt the weight of abandonment as he was cast into the pit by those who should have loved him. He is forsaken by his brothers, left to fend for himself in a foreign land, and seemingly forgotten by the God who gave him the dreams of future greatness. Yet, like the psalmist, Joseph does not abandon his faith in God. Though his circumstances are bleak, he continues to trust in God's plan, even when that plan seems incomprehensible.

Joseph's experience of being sold into slavery also echoes the themes of betrayal and abandonment that Christ Himself would experience. Just as Joseph was betrayed by his own brothers, Christ was betrayed by one of His closest followers, Judas. In both cases, the betrayal sets into motion a period of intense suffering, but it is suffering that ultimately leads to redemption. Joseph's time in slavery and imprisonment, like Christ's suffering on the cross, serves a greater purpose in God's redemptive plan.

Endurance In The Face Of False Accusation: The Righteous Sufferer's Integrity

After being sold into slavery, Joseph's suffering intensifies when he is falsely accused by Potiphar's wife. Though Joseph refuses her advances and acts with integrity, he is nevertheless accused of attempting to assault her and is thrown into prison. This false accusation is a profound injustice, compounding the suffering Joseph has already endured. He is not only betrayed by his family but now unjustly punished for a crime he did not commit.

Joseph's experience of being falsely accused mirrors the experience of the righteous sufferer in Psalm 22. In verses 6-7, the psalmist laments, "But I am a worm and not a man, scorned by everyone, despised by the people. All who see me mock me; they hurl insults, shaking their heads." Joseph's integrity, like that of the psalmist, is called into question, and he is despised and punished despite his innocence. Yet even in the face of this injustice, Joseph does not waver in his faith. He endures his suffering with patience, trusting that God is still in control.

This theme of unjust suffering and endurance in the face of false accusation also points forward to Christ, who was falsely accused and condemned to death despite His innocence. In Mark 14:55-59, we read of the chief priests and the Sanhedrin seeking false testimony against Jesus in order to put Him to death. Like

Joseph, Christ was accused of crimes He did not commit, and like Joseph, He endured His suffering with faith and trust in God's plan.

Joseph's ability to maintain his integrity and trust in God during this period of unjust suffering serves as a model for the righteous sufferer. It reminds us that suffering, though often unjust and difficult to understand, can be endured with faith and integrity. Joseph's experience teaches us that righteousness is not measured by the absence of suffering but by the ability to remain faithful to God in the midst of it.

Abandonment In Prison: The Righteous Sufferer's Cry For Deliverance

Perhaps the most poignant moment of Joseph's suffering comes during his time in prison. After being falsely accused and imprisoned, Joseph is seemingly forgotten by everyone, including the chief cupbearer whom he helps by interpreting his dream. In Genesis 40:23, we read, "The chief cupbearer, however, did not remember Joseph; he forgot him." Joseph's abandonment in prison echoes the cry of the psalmist in Psalm 22: "Why are you so far from saving me, so far from my cries of anguish?" (Psalm 22:1).

Joseph's time in prison represents the lowest point in his life. He is not only physically imprisoned but also emotionally and spiritually isolated. It is a time of deep suffering, where it would have been easy for Joseph to lose hope. And yet, despite this profound sense of abandonment, Joseph continues to trust in God. He does not allow his circumstances to dictate his faith, but instead remains steadfast, believing that God will deliver him in His own time.

This period of abandonment in Joseph's life mirrors the experience of the righteous sufferer in Psalm 22, who feels forsaken by God yet continues to cry out for deliverance. Joseph's endurance through this period of isolation and suffering foreshadows the endurance of Christ on the cross, who cried out, "My God, my God, why have you forsaken me?" (Matthew 27:46), yet trusted in the Father's plan for redemption. Like Christ, Joseph's suffering was not the end of the story; it was part of a larger narrative of redemption and deliverance.

The righteous sufferer, as seen in both Joseph and Christ, teaches us that feelings of abandonment are not incompatible with faith. In fact, the cry for deliverance, born out of a deep sense of isolation, is itself an act of faith. It is the recognition that even when God feels distant, He is still present, and His plan is still unfolding. Joseph's faith in the midst of abandonment serves as a model for all who endure suffering, reminding us that God's deliverance often comes in ways and at times we least expect.

Joseph's Vindication: The Righteous Sufferer's Deliverance And Exaltation

Joseph's story does not end in prison. After years of suffering, Joseph is finally vindicated when Pharaoh has a series of dreams that no one can interpret. The chief cupbearer, remembering Joseph's ability to interpret dreams, brings Joseph to Pharaoh, and Joseph successfully interprets the dreams as a warning of an impending famine. Impressed by Joseph's wisdom, Pharaoh elevates him to the second-highest position in Egypt, placing him in charge of preparing for the famine and distributing food.

This moment of vindication and exaltation parallels the conclusion of Psalm 22, where the psalmist, after lamenting his suffering, declares, "I will declare your name to my people; in the assembly I will praise you" (Psalm 22:22). The psalm, which begins with a cry of abandonment, ends with a declaration of praise and a promise of deliverance. Similarly, Joseph's story, which begins with betrayal and suffering, ends with his exaltation to a position of power and influence.

Joseph's vindication also points forward to the ultimate vindication and exaltation of Christ. After His crucifixion and death, Christ is raised from the dead and exalted to the right hand of the Father, where He reigns as King. In Philippians 2:9-11, Paul writes, "Therefore God exalted him to the highest place and gave him the name that is above every name, that at the name of Jesus every knee should bow, in heaven and on earth and under the earth, and every tongue acknowledge that Jesus Christ is Lord, to the glory of God the Father." Just as Joseph was exalted after his time of suffering, Christ was exalted after His crucifixion, and His exaltation brings about the ultimate deliverance for all who believe in Him.

Joseph's vindication reminds us that suffering is not the end of the story for the righteous. Like Joseph, the righteous sufferer may endure profound trials, but those trials ultimately lead to deliverance and exaltation. Joseph's story serves as a foreshadowing of the greater vindication and exaltation that Christ would experience, and it offers hope to all who endure suffering in this life, reminding us that God's plan for redemption is always at work, even in the darkest moments.

Joseph As A Model Of The Righteous Sufferer

As we reflect on Joseph's life in light of Psalm 22, we see a powerful connection between Joseph's experience as an innocent sufferer and the theme of the righteous sufferer in Scripture. Joseph's betrayal, false accusation, abandonment, and eventual vindication all serve as a type of the righteous sufferer, pointing forward to Christ's own experience on the cross. Like the psalmist in Psalm 22, Joseph endured profound suffering, yet he never wavered in his faith, trusting that God's plan for deliverance was still at work.

Joseph's life offers us a model of how to endure suffering with faith and integrity. His story reminds us that suffering is not a sign of God's absence but a part of His redemptive plan.

Like Joseph, we may experience betrayal, false accusation, and abandonment, but we can trust that God is still in control and that He will bring about our vindication in His own time.

Ultimately, Joseph's experience as a righteous sufferer points forward to Christ, the ultimate righteous sufferer, who endured the cross for the sake of our redemption. In both Joseph and Christ, we see the power of faith in the midst of suffering and the promise of deliverance for all who trust in God. As we face our own trials and suffering, may we follow their example, trusting that God's plan for redemption is always at work, even when we cannot see it.

Chapter 24: Study Questions For Reflection

Hope in the Face of Adversity

1. How does Joseph's story provide hope for those facing adversity?
2. What can we learn from Joseph's ability to trust in God despite his hardships?

CHAPTER 25: JOSEPH—A TYPE OF REDEMPTION AND CHRIST

As we bring this journey through the life of Joseph to a close, we find ourselves standing in awe of the profound ways his story intersects with the grand narrative of Scripture. Joseph's story is not merely a tale of personal perseverance or a record of historical events. It is a powerful prefiguration of the gospel message—a typology that connects his life to the ultimate redemption brought through Jesus Christ. From the moment Joseph appeared as the favored son of Jacob, marked by prophetic dreams, to his rise to power in Egypt and his ultimate reconciliation with his family, Joseph's life foreshadows God's redemptive work in ways that transcend time and place.

Joseph's story offers us an opportunity to see the hand of God, weaving together themes of suffering, forgiveness, preservation, intercession, and revelation, all of which find their fulfillment in Christ. Each chapter of Joseph's life points beyond itself, offering glimpses of the greater redemption that would come through the Messiah. As we reflect on these connections, we are reminded of the intricate ways in which God's sovereign plan unfolds across generations, culminating in the person and work of Jesus Christ.

Joseph As The Innocent Sufferer: A Prelude To Christ's Endurance

One of the most compelling themes in Joseph's life is his role as the innocent sufferer, a role that directly points to Christ's own suffering on the cross. Betrayed by his brothers, sold into slavery, falsely accused of a crime he did not commit, and abandoned in prison, Joseph endures profound injustice without losing his faith in God's plan. His story reflects the themes found in Psalm 22, where the righteous sufferer cries out to God in a moment of seeming abandonment, yet remains steadfast in trust.

Joseph's suffering begins at the hands of his own brothers. Their jealousy and hatred lead them to plot his downfall, culminating in the moment they throw him into a pit and sell him to traders bound for Egypt. This image of a beloved son betrayed by his family resonates deeply with the betrayal Christ endured. Jesus, too, was rejected by His own people. John 1:11 tells us, "He came to His own, and His own did not receive Him." The parallel is clear—both Joseph and Christ experienced profound rejection, not from strangers, but from those closest to them.

Yet, this suffering serves a greater purpose. Joseph's betrayal and suffering, while unjust, ultimately lead to the salvation of his family and the preservation of the nation of Israel. In the same way, Christ's suffering on the cross brought about the salvation of all humanity. Through His death and resurrection, Christ offers eternal life to those who place their trust in Him. Joseph's suffering prefigures the suffering of Christ, showing us that in God's economy, suffering is not wasted. It is often the crucible through which redemption and deliverance are brought forth.

The parallels between Joseph and Christ as innocent sufferers remind us that suffering is often part of God's redemptive plan. Through Joseph's life, we see that suffering, while painful, can serve a greater purpose, shaping the future and opening the way for God's deliverance. This theme encourages us to trust in God's sovereignty, even in the midst of trials, knowing that He can use our suffering for His glory and our good.

Forgiveness And Reconciliation: Joseph's Role As A Foreshadowing Of The New Covenant

One of the most profound moments in the biblical narrative is Joseph's act of forgiving his brothers after their betrayal. Despite the unimaginable wrongs done to him, Joseph chooses to forgive, seeing God's hand at work even in the midst of his suffering. This act of grace and reconciliation prefigures the forgiveness offered through the New Covenant, established through the sacrificial death of Christ.

Joseph's brothers, who once sold him into slavery, now stand before him, fearing retribution for their past sins. But Joseph, rather than seeking revenge, extends forgiveness, saying, "You intended to harm me, but God intended it for good to accomplish what is now being done, the saving of many lives" (Genesis 50:20). This moment of forgiveness is not just a personal act of mercy—it is a theological statement about the nature of God's redemptive plan. Joseph recognizes that his suffering had a purpose, one that went beyond personal vindication. God was at work, using even the evil intentions of his brothers to bring about salvation.

This act of forgiveness is a powerful foreshadowing of the grace that would come through Christ. In Jeremiah 31:31-34, we read of the New Covenant, in which God promises to forgive His people's sins and restore their relationship with Him. Joseph's willingness to forgive his brothers, to restore them to relationship, and to provide for their future mirrors the forgiveness offered through Christ. Just as Joseph's forgiveness brought healing to his family, Christ's forgiveness brings healing to our broken relationship with God, offering us the opportunity for reconciliation and new life.

Joseph's story, then, becomes a mirror of the New Covenant, a reflection of the grace and forgiveness that would one day be fully realized in Christ. This theme of forgiveness and reconciliation is central to the gospel message. In Christ, we are forgiven of our sins, not because we deserve it, but because of God's grace. And through this forgiveness, we are reconciled to God, restored to relationship with Him, and invited into the fullness of life that He offers.

Joseph As The Intercessor: A Picture Of Christ's Ongoing Mediation

Another key theme in Joseph's life is his role as an intercessor —between Pharaoh and the people of Egypt, and between his family and Pharaoh. Joseph's position of authority allowed him to mediate for those in need, ensuring that both the Egyptians and his own family were provided for during the famine.

When the famine struck, Joseph's brothers traveled to Egypt in search of food. Unbeknownst to them, the brother they had betrayed now held the keys to their survival. Joseph, as Pharaoh's right-hand man, had the power to grant or withhold provision. In this moment, Joseph serves as a mediator, standing between his family and the ruler of Egypt, advocating on their behalf and ensuring their survival. His position of authority allows him to intercede for those in need, securing their access to the resources they require to survive.

This role of intercession points forward to Christ's role as the ultimate mediator between humanity and God. Hebrews 7:25 tells us that Christ "always lives to intercede" for those who come to God through Him. Just as Joseph stood between two worlds—his Egyptian authority and his Hebrew heritage—Christ stands between heaven and earth, continually interceding on our behalf, securing our access to the Father and providing for our spiritual needs. Christ's role as our mediator ensures that we are never without an advocate before the throne of God.

Joseph's intercession during the famine offers us a glimpse of the greater work of intercession that Christ performs. Just as Joseph bridged the gap between his family and Pharaoh, Christ bridges the gap between humanity and God. Through His intercession, we receive the grace and mercy we need to navigate the spiritual famine of this world and find life in Him.

The Typology Of Preservation: Joseph And The Lineage Of Israel

Joseph's role in preserving the family of Israel during the famine is perhaps one of the most significant aspects of his story, particularly when viewed through the lens of typology. By providing refuge for his family in Egypt, Joseph ensures the survival of the line of Jacob—the very line from which the Messiah, Jesus, would one day come.

This theme of preservation speaks to God's faithfulness in fulfilling His promises, even in the face of overwhelming challenges. Throughout Israel's history, the lineage of David, from which the Messiah would come, was preserved despite numerous threats. Joseph's actions during the famine foreshadow this divine preservation, reminding us that God's plan for redemption is never in jeopardy, no matter the external circumstances.

In Genesis, we see how the preservation of Jacob's family was critical for the unfolding of God's covenant promises. Had Joseph not been in Egypt, prepared to provide for his family during the famine, the line of Israel might have been lost.

Instead, through Joseph's leadership and foresight, the family of Israel was preserved, and the covenantal promises made to Abraham, Isaac, and Jacob remained intact.

This preservation of the line of Israel points forward to Christ, who preserves our spiritual life. Just as Joseph ensured the survival of his family, Christ ensures the survival of His people. He sustains us through the trials of this world, guarding our faith and securing our eternal destiny. Jesus promises that "no one will snatch them out of my hand" (John 10:28). This theme of preservation is a reminder that our salvation is secure in Christ, not because of our strength, but because of His faithfulness.

Dreams And Revelation: Joseph As A Receiver And Interpreter Of God's Plan

Joseph's dreams, and his ability to interpret the dreams of others, play a central role in the unfolding of God's plan. From the beginning of his story, Joseph is marked by dreams that set him apart and foreshadow his future role. These dreams were not merely symbolic—they were prophetic revelations that guided Joseph's life and ensured the preservation of God's covenant people. In this sense, Joseph serves as a type of the prophetic tradition, through which God reveals His redemptive plan.

The typology of dreams in Joseph's life points forward to the greater revelation that would come through Christ, the one who reveals the fullness of God's redemptive plan. Just as Joseph's dreams foretold his future and guided his actions, the visions of Revelation in the New Testament reveal the ultimate fulfillment of God's plan for humanity. The dreams and visions given to Joseph were not random—they were part of God's unfolding plan to bring about salvation for His people.

Joseph's role as a receiver and interpreter of divine dreams invites us to see how God communicates His will throughout history. From the dreams of the patriarchs to the visions of the prophets, God has consistently used revelation to guide His people. This theme of revelation reaches its climax in Christ, who is the ultimate revelation of God's will and purpose. Hebrews 1:1-2 tells us that "in these last days [God] has spoken to us by his Son, whom he appointed heir of all things." In Christ, we see the fulfillment of all that God has revealed throughout history.

The Righteous Sufferer And The Exalted King: Joseph's Final Foreshadowing Of Christ

Joseph's story culminates in his exaltation to a position of power in Egypt, where he is given authority over the entire land and charged with saving the nation from famine. This moment of exaltation, following years of suffering and endurance, foreshadows the ultimate exaltation of Christ, who, after His death and resurrection, is seated at the right hand of the Father, reigning as King of Kings.

Joseph's journey from suffering to exaltation mirrors the journey of Christ, who, through His death and resurrection, triumphed over sin and death, bringing salvation to all who believe. Joseph's life offers us a glimpse of the greater redemptive plan that would unfold through Christ. Just as Joseph was elevated to a position of authority in Egypt, Christ was exalted to the highest place in heaven, where He reigns as the sovereign King over all creation.

This theme of exaltation reminds us that suffering is not the end of the story—it is the prelude to exaltation and victory. Joseph's life, marked by suffering and endurance, points forward to the greater victory that would come through Christ's resurrection and ascension. In both Joseph's story and Christ's, we see the pattern of suffering followed by exaltation, reminding us that God's redemptive purposes often unfold in ways that defy our expectations.

Joseph As A Type Of Redemption

In Joseph's life, we see a powerful type of Christ—a foreshadowing of the redemption that would come through the Messiah. His suffering, his forgiveness, his role as an intercessor and preserver, and his exaltation all point forward to the greater work of redemption that Christ would accomplish on the cross. Through Joseph, we catch a glimpse of God's redemptive plan, a plan that would unfold over centuries and find its fulfillment in Jesus Christ.

As we conclude this journey through Joseph's life, we are reminded of the profound ways in which God's plan for redemption is woven throughout Scripture. Joseph's story is not just a narrative of personal triumph—it is a story of God's faithfulness, His grace, and His unwavering commitment to bring about the salvation of His people. And in Christ, we see the ultimate fulfillment of that plan, as God's redemptive purposes are fully revealed and brought to completion.

Joseph's life invites us to trust in the sovereignty of God, to endure suffering with faith, and to embrace the forgiveness and reconciliation that comes through Christ. As we reflect on Joseph's journey, may we be encouraged to see our own lives as part of this greater redemptive story, trusting that God is at work, even in the midst of our trials, to bring about His purposes for our good and His glory.

Chapter 25: Study Questions For Reflection

The Final Reconciliation:

1. How does the final reconciliation between Joseph and his brothers mirror God's reconciliation with humanity?
2. What does Joseph's story teach us about God's desire for unity within families and communities?

EPILOGUE

Call to Action: Living in the Light of Redemption

Joseph's life is not just a story from ancient history; it's a living example of God's faithfulness, grace, and redemptive power. His journey, marked by betrayal, suffering, and ultimate triumph, reflects the path we, too, are called to walk. Like Joseph, we are often tested, faced with trials, and called to endure circumstances that seem beyond our control. Yet, through it all, God is working—sometimes behind the scenes, but always with purpose.

The story of Joseph calls us to something more than passive reflection. It invites us into action, challenging us to live out the truths of faith, endurance, and reconciliation that his life exemplifies. Just as Joseph trusted in God's plan, even when it seemed like everything was against him, we too must trust that God is weaving a greater story in our own lives—one that will ultimately lead to His glory and our good.

Now is the time to ask yourself: where is God calling you to trust Him more deeply? What areas of your life need the kind of forgiveness Joseph extended to his brothers? How can you live in light of the redemption that Christ has offered, not only for your own salvation but as a vessel of His grace to others?

Trust In God's Sovereignty

Joseph's life reminds us that no matter how dark our circumstances may seem, God is sovereign. He is present in our struggles, working all things together for good. Trust Him, even when you cannot see the way forward. Let your faith in His promises guide you through every trial, knowing that His plans for you are greater than you can imagine.

Embrace Forgiveness And Reconciliation

Like Joseph, we are called to be agents of reconciliation. Whether it's in our relationships with family, friends, or even ourselves, forgiveness is the key to healing and restoration. Christ has extended forgiveness to us; now it is our turn to extend that same grace to those who have wronged us. Let go of bitterness, choose to forgive, and allow God to bring reconciliation where there was once brokenness.

STEP INTO YOUR ROLE AS AN INTERCESSOR

Just as Joseph interceded on behalf of his family and the people of Egypt, we are called to intercede for others. Pray for those around you—your family, your community, your world. Stand in the gap, seeking God's provision, grace, and healing for others. Through your prayers and actions, you can be a channel of God's blessings, helping to preserve and uplift those in need.

Live With Purpose And Expectation

Joseph's dreams were not just for himself; they were part of God's larger plan for the salvation of many. In the same way, God has a purpose for your life that goes beyond your immediate circumstances. Live with expectation that He will fulfill His promises. Step boldly into the future, knowing that your story, like Joseph's, is part of a much greater narrative—the redemption of all creation through Christ.

Be A Beacon Of Hope And Redemption

The world is full of brokenness, but as followers of Christ, we are called to be lights in the darkness. Joseph's story shows us that no matter how far we've fallen or how great the obstacles we face, God's redemptive power can transform everything.

Let your life be a testimony of this truth. Share the hope of redemption with those around you, not only in words but through your actions—through kindness, generosity, and love.

The Invitation To Walk In Faith

You are not merely a spectator in the story of redemption; you are an active participant. As you close this book and reflect on Joseph's life, the call is clear: trust in God's sovereignty, forgive as you have been forgiven, and walk in the light of Christ's redemption. Just as Joseph's journey of faith and endurance led to the salvation of many, your journey, too, has the potential to impact lives for generations to come.

Now is the time to step forward in faith, knowing that God is with you, guiding your path, and using your life for His greater purpose. Answer the call. Live in the light of redemption. Trust in the God who never fails.

RECEIVING JESUS: A PATH TO ETERNAL LIFE

The message of salvation through Jesus Christ is the foundation of the Christian faith. God, in His love and grace, has made a way for every person to be reconciled to Him, forgiven of their sins, and receive the gift of eternal life. This invitation is open to everyone, regardless of their past or present circumstances. Salvation is not earned by good works or religious rituals but is a gift of God's grace, received by faith in Jesus Christ.

Why Do We Need Salvation?

The Bible teaches that every human being has sinned and fallen short of God's perfect standard. Sin separates us from God and brings spiritual death (Romans 3:23; Romans 6:23). We cannot bridge the gap between ourselves and God through our own efforts. However, God, in His great love, sent His Son, Jesus Christ, to pay the penalty for our sins by dying on the cross. Jesus' death and resurrection made it possible for us to be forgiven and reconciled to God.

The Good News: Jesus Saves

The gospel (good news) is that Jesus Christ died for our sins, was buried, and rose again on the third day (1 Corinthians 15:3-4). Through His sacrifice, Jesus paid the price for our sins and offers us the gift of eternal life. Jesus Himself said, "I am the way and the truth and the life. No one comes to the Father except through me" (John 14:6).

Salvation is a free gift. It is not based on how good you are or what you've done in the past. It is given freely to anyone who believes in Jesus and trusts Him for the forgiveness of their sins.

Steps To Accept Jesus And Receive Salvation

1. **Acknowledge Your Need for Salvation**
   The first step is recognizing that you need a Savior. We all have sinned, and no matter how hard we try, we cannot save ourselves. Acknowledge that you are separated from God because of sin and need His forgiveness.

"For all have sinned and fall short of the glory of God" (Romans 3:23).

2. **Believe in Jesus Christ**
   Believe that Jesus is the Son of God, that He died on the cross for your sins, and that He rose from the dead to give you new life. This belief is more than intellectual—it's trusting in Jesus as the only way to be saved and reconciled to God.

"Believe in the Lord Jesus, and you will be saved" (Acts 16:31).

3. **Repent of Your Sins**
   Repentance means turning away from your sins and turning toward God. It's not just feeling sorry for your

sins but making a decision to change direction in your life. Ask God to forgive you and help you live according to His will.

"Repent, then, and turn to God, so that your sins may be wiped out, that times of refreshing may come from the Lord" (Acts 3:19).

4. **Confess Jesus as Lord**
   Confessing Jesus as Lord means acknowledging that He is the ruler of your life. It's a declaration of your faith and a commitment to follow Him. When you confess Jesus as Lord, you are committing your life to Him and accepting His leadership.

"If you declare with your mouth, 'Jesus is Lord,' and believe in your heart that God raised him from the dead, you will be saved" (Romans 10:9).

5. **Receive the Gift of Salvation by Faith**
   Salvation is a gift from God, and we receive it through faith. You don't have to earn it or work for it—just believe and receive it by faith. Trust that God has forgiven your sins and that you are now a new creation in Christ.

"For it is by grace you have been saved, through faith—and this is not from yourselves, it is the gift of God—not by works, so that no one can boast" (Ephesians 2:8-9).

Pray To Accept Jesus

If you are ready to accept Jesus Christ as your Lord and Savior, you can pray a simple prayer like this from your heart:

> Dear Heavenly Father,
>
> I come to You just as I am, knowing that I am a sinner in need of Your forgiveness. I believe that Jesus Christ is Your Son, that He died on the cross for my sins, and that You raised Him from the dead. Right now, I ask You to forgive my sins and come into my heart, Lord Jesus. I turn from my past and surrender my life to You. I want to trust You as my Savior and follow You as my Lord from this moment forward.
>
> Thank You for loving me, for dying for me, and for the gift of eternal life. Help me to live for You every day and grow in my faith. I ask You to fill me with Your Holy Spirit and guide me in the path You have for me. In Jesus' name, I pray. Amen.

What Happens Next?

If you've prayed this prayer and accepted Jesus as your Savior, the Bible says you are now a child of God! Your sins are forgiven, and you have a new life in Christ (2 Corinthians 5:17). This is the beginning of a lifelong journey of growing in faith, learning more about God, and living according to His Word.

Here are a few steps to help you grow in your new relationship with God:

1. **Read the Bible**
   The Bible is God's Word, and it will help you understand more about His love, His promises, and His plan for your life. Start with the Gospels (Matthew, Mark, Luke, and John) to learn more about Jesus.

2. **Pray Regularly**
   Prayer is simply talking to God. Spend time every day thanking Him, asking for guidance, and sharing your thoughts and concerns. God loves to hear from you.

3. **Find a Church Community**
   Being part of a local church will help you grow in your faith and provide support from other believers. A church community can encourage you, pray for you, and help you learn more about following Jesus.

4. **Tell Others About Your Faith**
   Share your story of how you came to faith in Jesus. Telling others about what Jesus has done for you is a natural way to express your gratitude and encourage others to find the same hope and salvation.

Accepting Jesus and becoming saved is the most important decision you can make, and it's the beginning of a new and abundant life with God. You are not alone—God is with you every step of the way, guiding and loving you as you grow in your relationship with Him.

This doesn't mean that you won't sin or that you'll suddenly become perfect. In reality, our righteousness comes from Jesus, not from anything we do on our own. We are considered sinless and blameless before God because He is sinless, and His perfection covers us. It is through His sacrifice that we are made right with God, not by our own strength or works.

As you continue to walk this path of faith, remember that your relationship with Christ is what defines you, not your failures. When you stumble, turn to Him, knowing that His grace is always sufficient. He is your righteousness, your strength, and your guide every step of the way. Trust in His grace, and let His love sustain you as you grow and learn to live in His light.

GLOSSARY OF TERMS

Atonement

The act of reconciliation between God and humanity, achieved through the sacrificial death of Jesus Christ. In Joseph's story, atonement is symbolized through acts of forgiveness and reconciliation with his brothers.

Christ

The Greek term for "Messiah," meaning "anointed one." Jesus Christ is regarded as the promised deliverer and Savior of humanity in Christian belief, fulfilling God's plan of redemption.

Covenant

A solemn agreement between God and humanity, often involving specific promises and obligations. The New Covenant, established through Jesus Christ, promises the forgiveness of sins and eternal life to all who believe.

Divine Providence

The belief that God governs and sustains the universe and human history according to His will and purpose. In Joseph's life, Divine Providence is evident as God guides his trials and triumphs for a greater purpose.

Exaltation

The act of raising someone to a higher rank or position. In Christian theology, it refers to Jesus Christ being raised from the dead and seated at the right hand of God, reigning as King of Kings. Joseph's rise to power in Egypt is a typological foreshadowing of Christ's exaltation.

Faithfulness

Loyalty and steadfast trust in God, even amidst trials. Joseph's faithfulness throughout his hardships exemplifies the commitment to trust in God's purpose and timing.

Famine
A period of extreme scarcity of food. In Joseph's story, the famine in Egypt is central to his rise to leadership and symbolizes God's provision during times of scarcity.

Forgiveness
The act of pardoning an offense or wrongdoing. Central to the narrative of Joseph and the New Covenant, forgiveness is a key aspect of Christian doctrine, where God forgives humanity's sins through Christ's sacrifice.

Intercession
The act of intervening or mediating on behalf of others, especially in prayer. In the Bible, Jesus is seen as the ultimate intercessor between humanity and God. Joseph's role as a mediator during the famine reflects this intercessory role.

Messiah
A term meaning "the anointed one," prophesied in the Old Testament to be the deliverer of the Jewish people. Christians believe Jesus is the Messiah who brings salvation not just to Israel, but to all humanity.

New Covenant
The covenant established through Jesus Christ, promising the forgiveness of sins and the gift of eternal life to all who have faith in Him. It is the fulfillment of the Old Testament prophecies of restoration and reconciliation with God.

Divine Revelation
The act by which God reveals His will, truth, or purpose to humanity. Joseph's gift of interpreting dreams is a form of divine revelation, guiding him in the role God prepared for him.

Preservation
The act of maintaining or safeguarding something. In Joseph's

story, preservation refers to his role in saving his family and the future nation of Israel from famine. It also prefigures Christ's preservation of the spiritual life of believers.

Prophecy

A message or prediction revealed by God, often foretelling future events or divine plans. Joseph's dreams are prophetic, foreshadowing his future and the preservation of his family, aligning with biblical prophecy.

Reconciliation

The restoration of a broken relationship. In Joseph's story, reconciliation occurs when he forgives his brothers and restores their relationship. This mirrors the reconciliation between God and humanity offered through Jesus Christ.

Redemption

The act of being saved from sin or evil, often involving a price being paid. In Christian theology, redemption refers to Christ's sacrificial death on the cross to save humanity from sin and its consequences. Joseph's life serves as a foreshadowing of this ultimate act of redemption.

Resurrection

The belief in rising from the dead. In Christian faith, Jesus Christ's resurrection is central, signifying His victory over sin and death. Joseph's rise from the depths of suffering to power mirrors this theme of resurrection.

Salvation

The deliverance from sin and its consequences, granted by God through faith in Jesus Christ. Joseph's actions in saving his family from famine foreshadow the salvation offered to all through Christ.

Sovereignty

God's supreme authority and control over all creation. The sovereignty of God is a key theme in Joseph's life, as God's will prevails despite human actions, guiding events for the fulfillment of His redemptive plan.

Suffering Servant
A figure in the Old Testament, particularly in the book of Isaiah, who endures suffering on behalf of others. Joseph's suffering and eventual triumph serve as a type of the Suffering Servant, prefiguring Christ's suffering and sacrifice.

Typology
A theological concept where events, persons, or institutions in the Old Testament prefigure or foreshadow greater realities fulfilled in the New Testament. Joseph's life is typologically connected to Christ, serving as a precursor to the redemptive work of Jesus.

Dream Interpretation
The process of understanding the meaning of dreams, often involving divine messages. In Joseph's story, his interpretations reveal God's guidance and play a key role in saving Egypt and his family.

SUGGESTED READING

These resources have been invaluable to me in exploring the themes of Joseph's story and its prophetic significance. Each of these works offers deep insights into biblical prophecy, theology, and scriptural interpretation. They provide essential background and context that enrich our understanding of God's redemptive plan as revealed in both the Old and New Testaments.

G.K. Beale, *The Book of Revelation: A Commentary on the Greek Text*
This comprehensive commentary offers an in-depth analysis of the Book of Revelation, focusing on its original Greek text. Beale's scholarly work is invaluable for understanding the complex symbolism and themes within Revelation.

Francis Brown, S.R. Driver, and Charles A. Briggs, *A Hebrew and English Lexicon of the Old Testament*
Commonly known as "BDB," this lexicon is a foundational resource for studying the Hebrew language of the Old Testament. It provides detailed definitions and explanations of Hebrew words, aiding in deeper scriptural understanding.

David J.A. Clines, ed., *The Dictionary of Classical Hebrew*
This multi-volume dictionary offers an exhaustive compilation of Hebrew words found in the Old Testament, providing insights into their meanings and usage. It's an essential tool for serious Hebrew language scholars.

Victor P. Hamilton, *The Book of Genesis, Chapters 18–50*
Part of the New International Commentary on the Old Testament series, Hamilton's work provides a thorough

examination of the latter chapters of Genesis, offering historical context and theological insights.

Craig S. Keener, *The IVP Bible Background Commentary: New Testament*
Keener's commentary sheds light on the cultural, historical, and social contexts of the New Testament writings, enhancing comprehension of the scriptures.

Leon Morris, *The Revelation of St. John: An Introduction and Commentary*
Morris offers a clear and concise commentary on the Book of Revelation, making its complex themes accessible to readers. His work is part of the Tyndale New Testament Commentaries series.

John H. Sailhamer, *The Pentateuch as Narrative: A Biblical-Theological Commentary*
Sailhamer presents the first five books of the Bible as a unified narrative, exploring their theological themes and literary structure.

Bruce K. Waltke and Cathi J. Fredricks, *Genesis: A Commentary*
This commentary provides an in-depth analysis of the Book of Genesis, combining scholarly research with accessible writing.

N.T. Wright, *Jesus and the Victory of God*
Wright's work is a comprehensive study of Jesus's life and ministry, offering insights into his role within the context of first-century Judaism and early Christianity.

GUIDED REFLECTIONS

Chapter 1: Favored Son, Betrayed Brother

1. **Joseph's early life reflects spiritual trials** when God sets us apart for a purpose. His favored status caused jealousy, showing that being chosen can sometimes bring isolation and challenges from others.
2. **Jealousy and envy** can cause divisions in families and communities. Joseph's brothers allowed their resentment to lead to betrayal, demonstrating how unchecked emotions can destroy relationships.
3. **Betrayal is painful**, but it often opens doors for God's greater plan. Joseph's betrayal led him into God's purpose, showing that God works through even the most difficult circumstances.
4. **Joseph's dreams** were a revelation of God's sovereign plan. They foreshadowed his rise to power and his eventual role in saving his family, showing that God's plan prevails even in adversity.

Chapter 2: The Pit And The 6Th Seal—Shaken But Not Destroyed

1. **Joseph's experience in the pit** is symbolic of the dark periods in our lives. We may feel abandoned or hopeless, but these times are often the foundation for future growth.

2. **Cosmic upheaval parallels personal trials**, shaking our sense of security. Like Joseph, we are called to trust God's purposes, even when everything seems to be falling apart.
3. **Enduring faith** is demonstrated by Joseph, who remained faithful despite betrayal and slavery. This teaches us that our response to trials should be rooted in trusting God's greater plan.
4. **God uses trials to prepare us** for future roles. Just as Joseph's hardship prepared him for leadership in Egypt, our own struggles can shape us for the work God has planned.

Chapter 3: From Prison To Power—The Endurance Of The Saints

1. **Believers face challenges** that test their endurance, much like Joseph's imprisonment. His faith through injustice is a model for enduring in faith, even when life seems unfair.
2. **Joseph's faithfulness in prison** teaches us to remain diligent and faithful in every circumstance, trusting that God sees our integrity and will reward it in His time.
3. **Periods of waiting**, like Joseph's time in prison, often feel like we've been forgotten. But these are moments where God is preparing us for something greater, as He did for Joseph.
4. **God's timing is perfect**, even when it feels delayed. Joseph's rise to power came at the right moment, showing us that enduring hardship leads to God's greater plan being revealed.

Chapter 4: Managing The Famine—The Wisdom Of Joseph

1. **Joseph's wisdom in managing the famine** shows how God provides in times of crisis. His leadership saved countless lives, emphasizing the importance of planning and foresight.
2. **Preparation and stewardship** are essential lessons. Joseph's careful management of resources during abundance teaches us to prepare both spiritually and materially for future hardships.
3. **Responding to abundance with gratitude and responsibility** helps us prepare for times of need. By storing up faith and resources, we can face challenges with confidence.
4. **Generosity and wise leadership** go hand in hand. Joseph's ability to provide for others despite his personal hardships is a model for us to use our blessings to help those in need.
5. **Trust in God's guidance** is key to navigating crises. Joseph trusted in the interpretation of Pharaoh's dreams and acted on it, showing that divine guidance equips us for leadership during difficult times.

Chapter 5: The Feast Of Atonement—Forgiveness And Reconciliation

1. **Joseph's forgiveness of his brothers** reflects the heart of the Atonement—God's desire to restore broken relationships through repentance and forgiveness.
2. **Reconciliation is a process**, as Joseph tested his brothers to see if they had truly changed. True

reconciliation requires repentance and a willingness to be tested.

3. **Personal experiences of forgiveness** can be transformative, both for the person offering it and the one receiving it. Like Joseph, forgiving others opens the way for healing and restoration.

4. **Humility is essential** in seeking and giving forgiveness. Joseph's brothers had to humble themselves, just as we must humble ourselves before God and others to receive true reconciliation.

5. **Joseph's grace** towards his brothers is a reflection of God's grace toward us. It challenges us to extend forgiveness, even in situations of deep hurt or betrayal.

6. **The Feast of Atonement** calls us to reconcile with God and others. Joseph's family's restoration reminds us of the importance of mending relationships and seeking God's mercy.

Chapter 6: Restoration Of The Family—The Spiritual Temple

1. **God desires to restore relationships**, as seen in Joseph's reconciliation with his family. This mirrors God's longing to restore His relationship with humanity through Christ.

2. **Forgiveness and grace** were pivotal in healing Joseph's family. Without Joseph's willingness to forgive, restoration would have been impossible. It teaches us that grace is the foundation for mending brokenness.

3. **Trials often lead to restoration**. Joseph's suffering led to the reunification of his family, showing us that periods of separation or hardship can be the precursor to healing and restoration.

4. **Joseph's family restoration foreshadows Christ's spiritual restoration** of His people. Just as Joseph saved his family, Christ redeems and restores those who come to Him.

5. **The spiritual temple** refers to our relationship with God, where He restores and builds us into His spiritual house. Allowing God to restore us spiritually is crucial for our personal growth.

6. **Joseph's reunion with Jacob** is a powerful picture of God's desire to reunite with His people. It shows that no matter how far we stray, God desires reconciliation and will provide a way for restoration.

Chapter 7: Joseph—A Life Of Endurance, Preparation, And Reconciliation

1. **Endurance is key** to trusting in God's timing. Like Joseph, we must hold fast to faith, knowing that trials are temporary and are leading us to God's greater plan.

2. **Joseph's preparation during abundance** teaches us to wisely steward the resources and opportunities God gives us. Whether spiritual or material, preparation helps us navigate difficult seasons.

3. **Reconciliation is a powerful theme**, both in Joseph's life and in our own. Whether with family, friends, or God, the process of healing and restoring relationships brings peace and fulfillment.

4. **Trials shape us** for future roles. Just as Joseph's character was developed through hardship, our own faith is refined during tough times, preparing us for what God has planned.

5. **Joseph's faithfulness** in all circumstances, whether in prison or in power, teaches us that trusting in God's

providence is the foundation of a life of integrity and purpose.

6. **Endurance, preparation, and reconciliation** are lifelong processes. God is constantly at work, refining us, equipping us, and calling us to seek restoration in all areas of life.

Chapter 8: Reflecting On Joseph's Life And Trials —A Foreshadowing Of The 6Th Seal

1. **How does Joseph's personal journey of betrayal, suffering, and redemption foreshadow the events described in the 6th Seal?**
    - Joseph's life parallels the events of the 6th Seal in that both involve a period of great tribulation, where everything seems to be falling apart. In Joseph's case, his betrayal by his brothers, descent into slavery, and unjust imprisonment mirror the cosmic upheaval described in Revelation 6:12-14, where the earth quakes, the sun darkens, and stars fall. These moments of shaking in both Joseph's life and the 6th Seal serve as precursors to a greater plan of redemption. Just as Joseph's trials led to his eventual rise to power and the salvation of his family, the events of the 6th Seal lead to the unfolding of God's final plan for humanity.

2. **Joseph's endurance through tribulation is a central theme in his story. How can Joseph's example of faithfulness inspire us to endure during times of spiritual testing or hardship?**
    - Joseph's faithfulness in the face of extreme hardship is a powerful example of enduring

faith. Despite being betrayed by his family, falsely accused, and imprisoned, Joseph remained steadfast in his trust in God's plan. He never allowed bitterness or despair to take root in his heart. His ability to trust God in the midst of suffering shows us that even in our darkest moments, we can cling to God's promises, knowing that He is working behind the scenes for our good. This same endurance is called for in times of spiritual testing, especially during the trials foretold in the 6th Seal.

3. **In both Joseph's life and the 6th Seal, we see moments of great shaking that lead to a greater purpose. How can we find hope in the idea that God uses times of upheaval to bring about His divine plan?**
    - We can find hope in the fact that God often uses periods of upheaval to bring about transformation and redemption. Just as Joseph's betrayal and imprisonment were not the end of his story but part of a larger divine plan, the tribulations described in the 6th Seal are not a sign of defeat but of preparation for God's ultimate victory. Knowing that God is in control even in times of chaos allows us to trust that He is using our trials to shape us for a greater purpose. This perspective gives us hope that what seems like destruction or loss is often the foundation for God's redemptive work.

4. **Joseph's trials were a form of preparation for his eventual rise to power. How can we, as believers, prepare for the tribulations described in the 6th Seal?**
    - Joseph's ability to remain faithful during his trials served as preparation for his eventual

leadership role in Egypt. As believers, we can prepare for future tribulations by deepening our relationship with God, strengthening our faith, and cultivating trust in His sovereignty. We can also prepare by studying Scripture, seeking God's wisdom, and relying on the Holy Spirit for guidance. Joseph's example teaches us that preparation involves both spiritual resilience and practical readiness, trusting that God will provide what we need to endure and overcome challenges.

5. **The theme of reconciliation is central to both Joseph's story and God's ultimate plan for humanity. How does Joseph's reconciliation with his brothers reflect God's desire to reconcile with His people through Christ?**
   - Joseph's willingness to forgive his brothers and reconcile with them after years of separation mirrors God's desire to reconcile with humanity through Christ. Just as Joseph extended grace to those who wronged him, God extends grace to us, offering forgiveness and restoration through the sacrifice of Christ. This reconciliation is not just a mending of broken relationships but a demonstration of God's love and His redemptive plan to bring His people back into communion with Him. Joseph's story reflects the heart of God, who seeks to heal the divisions caused by sin and restore His people through His grace.

6. **As we reflect on Joseph's story as a foreshadowing of the 6th Seal, how does this help us understand the nature of suffering and God's sovereignty?**
   - Joseph's life helps us understand that

suffering is often part of God's larger plan, a means by which He brings about transformation and redemption. The 6th Seal, like Joseph's trials, reveals that tribulation is not arbitrary but serves a divine purpose. Through suffering, God refines us, preparing us for the fulfillment of His promises. Understanding God's sovereignty means recognizing that He is in control even when circumstances seem chaotic or unjust. Just as God used Joseph's suffering to save his family and many others, He uses the tribulations of the 6th Seal to bring about His ultimate plan for the salvation of humanity.

Chapter 9: Joseph's Journey From Suffering To Sovereignty

1. **What does Joseph's journey teach us about enduring suffering and hardship?**
    - Joseph's journey exemplifies resilience in the face of adversity. Despite being sold into slavery and later imprisoned unjustly, he continued to trust in God. His steadfastness teaches us that enduring hardship is part of God's greater purpose, shaping us and preparing us for future roles of influence and service.
2. **How does Joseph's story illustrate God's providence and timing?**
    - Joseph's rise to power at precisely the right time to interpret Pharaoh's dreams and prepare for the famine reflects God's perfect timing. It shows that, while we may

not understand our trials, God orchestrates events for the ultimate good, aligning them with His divine plan for salvation and provision.

3. **What role does forgiveness play in Joseph's life, and how can this be applied to our lives?**
    - Joseph's forgiveness of his brothers, despite their betrayal, highlights the power of grace and reconciliation. He recognized God's hand in his suffering and extended mercy instead of revenge. This teaches us to seek forgiveness and reconciliation, even in difficult circumstances, as a reflection of God's redemptive work.

4. **How does Joseph's role as a savior in Egypt foreshadow Christ's role as Savior?**
    - Joseph saved Egypt and his family from famine through his wisdom and preparation, mirroring Christ's role in providing salvation to humanity. Just as Joseph became a source of sustenance and life, Christ offers spiritual sustenance and reconciliation with God, becoming the ultimate provider for our deepest needs.

5. **What can we learn about preparation from Joseph's actions during the years of abundance?**
    - Joseph's foresight in storing grain during years of plenty teaches the importance of preparation, both physically and spiritually. His wisdom ensured survival during the famine, highlighting the value of planning and readiness for future trials. For believers, this serves as a reminder to cultivate faith and resilience in prosperous times to endure hardships.

6. **In what ways did Joseph's suffering and subsequent exaltation foreshadow the suffering and resurrection of Christ?**
    - Joseph's descent into suffering, followed by his rise to power, parallels Christ's journey from the cross to resurrection. Joseph's endurance through betrayal and hardship paved the way for his role as a savior figure in Egypt, just as Christ's suffering and resurrection opened the way to eternal life for all believers.

Chapter 10: Joseph: A Type of the 6th Seal and the Feasts

1. **How does Joseph's decision to forgive his brothers reflect the spirit of the Feast of Atonement, which focuses on repentance and reconciliation with God?**
    - Joseph's forgiveness mirrors the essence of the Feast of Atonement by highlighting the themes of repentance, forgiveness, and reconciliation. Just as the feast calls for introspection and the seeking of forgiveness, Joseph's decision to forgive his brothers after testing their hearts emphasizes the power of mercy and grace to restore broken relationships. His forgiveness reflects God's desire to reconcile with humanity, even when we have wronged Him.
2. **In what ways does Joseph test his brothers' hearts before fully reconciling with them? What does this teach us about the process of genuine reconciliation?**
    - Joseph tests his brothers by observing their reactions to his accusations and by asking them to bring Benjamin, which reveals whether they have changed since selling him into slavery. This process shows that genuine reconciliation often requires honest evaluation and accountability,

ensuring that the repentance is sincere. It teaches that true reconciliation involves both parties acknowledging past wrongs and working toward mutual understanding.

3. **Reflect on a time when you were in need of forgiveness or when you extended forgiveness to someone else. How did the process of reconciliation impact you or the other person involved?**
    - Personal responses will vary, but often the process of seeking or offering forgiveness brings relief, closure, and the opportunity for growth in both parties. Reconciliation can deepen relationships, fostering trust and compassion, as it allows individuals to move beyond past hurts with a renewed sense of peace and connection.

4. **What role does humility play in both giving and receiving forgiveness, as seen in the interactions between Joseph and his brothers?**
    - Humility is central in Joseph's forgiveness of his brothers and in their repentance. Joseph, despite his high status, approaches his family with a compassionate and forgiving heart. Similarly, his brothers demonstrate humility by admitting their past wrongs and expressing regret. Humility allows both parties to put aside pride, accept responsibility, and pursue healing in relationships.

5. **How can we apply Joseph's example of grace and forgiveness to relationships in our own lives, particularly in situations where we have been deeply hurt or betrayed?**
    - Joseph's example teaches us that grace and forgiveness can bring healing even in the most painful situations. By choosing to forgive rather than seek revenge, we can break cycles of hurt and bitterness. Applying grace involves seeing

the bigger picture, recognizing that forgiveness often frees both the forgiver and the forgiven, allowing for new beginnings and restored relationships.

6. **The Feast of Atonement is about restoring relationships with God and with others. How can you seek to reconcile broken relationships in your life and draw closer to God in the process?**
    - Reconciling broken relationships requires a willingness to forgive, to seek forgiveness, and to communicate openly. Through prayer, self-reflection, and humility, individuals can address hurts and work toward rebuilding trust. In doing so, they not only heal relationships with others but also strengthen their connection to God, who calls for unity, forgiveness, and peace within His family.

Chapter 11: Restoration Of The Family—The Spiritual Temple

1. **How does Joseph's restoration of his family reflect God's desire to restore broken relationships with His people?**
    - Joseph's willingness to forgive his brothers and restore their relationship reflects God's heart for reconciliation. Just as Joseph welcomed his brothers back with love, God seeks to heal and restore His relationship with humanity, offering forgiveness and grace through Christ.
2. **What role does forgiveness and grace play in the healing of Joseph's family? How can you apply these principles to relationships in your life?**

- Forgiveness and grace are essential for healing and restoring relationships. Joseph's grace allowed his brothers to reconcile without fear, exemplifying the power of forgiveness to transform lives. Applying these principles in our lives involves forgiving others as God forgives us, fostering healing in strained relationships.

3. **In what ways have you experienced restoration in your life after a season of trial?**
    - Personal reflections will vary, but restoration often comes after repentance, forgiveness, and God's intervention. Like Joseph's family reunion, God brings healing and unity through His love, especially after periods of hardship.

Chapter 12: The Unveiling Of God's Plan—From Hidden To Revealed And The Feast Of Atonement—Forgiveness And Reconciliation

1. **How does Joseph's story illustrate the way God's plan can remain hidden and gradually unfold over time? Reflect on a time when you experienced a hidden purpose that was later revealed.**
    - Joseph's life demonstrates that God's plans often unfold in stages, revealing pieces of His purpose through dreams, trials, and opportunities. His early dreams hinted at his future but didn't reveal the full path, especially his suffering and eventual rise to power. Similarly, in our lives, we may not understand the reasons behind our challenges until later, when God reveals how they fit

into His bigger picture. Personally, moments of confusion or hardship often make sense in retrospect, showing God's hand at work.

2. **What lessons can we learn from Joseph's response to his trials regarding faith and trust in God's timing?**
   - Joseph's patient endurance throughout slavery and imprisonment shows his unwavering faith in God's timing. He trusted that God would fulfill His promises, even when circumstances seemed bleak. This teaches us to hold onto faith and trust that God's timing is perfect, even if we face prolonged hardship or delay.

3. **In what ways do Joseph's early dreams serve as a "glimpse" of God's greater plan for his life? How do they shape his journey despite the challenges he faces?**
   - Joseph's dreams foreshadowed his future role in leading and preserving his family, offering him an early vision of God's purpose. Though his brothers misunderstood the dreams as arrogance, they gave Joseph a sense of destiny that likely strengthened his resolve. These glimpses of God's plan can offer us hope and perspective when we face setbacks, helping us focus on a higher purpose.

4. **How does the theme of hiddenness in Joseph's life connect to the idea of the Feast of Atonement, where God calls His people to self-examination and reconciliation?**
   - Just as Joseph's journey involved hidden trials that later revealed God's purpose, the Feast of Atonement is a time of self-examination, where individuals confront hidden sins and seek reconciliation. This hiddenness serves as

a reminder that God often works behind the scenes, calling us to examine our hearts and address broken relationships as part of His larger plan for restoration.

5. **Why was it important for Joseph to test his brothers before revealing his identity, and how does this process relate to the deeper purpose of repentance and reconciliation?**
    - Joseph's tests allowed him to see whether his brothers had truly repented and changed. By observing their actions, he could assess their integrity and willingness to protect Benjamin. This process mirrors the steps of true repentance, where genuine change is demonstrated through actions, setting the stage for reconciliation based on honesty and transformation.

6. **How does Joseph's forgiveness of his brothers serve as a model for us, especially in light of the themes of the Feast of Atonement? How can we practice forgiveness and reconciliation in our own relationships?**
    - Joseph's forgiveness shows a depth of grace and mercy that transcends his personal hurt. He forgave his brothers, recognizing God's larger purpose. This aligns with the Feast of Atonement's call to forgive and be reconciled. Practicing forgiveness in our lives requires humility, seeing beyond offenses, and being willing to restore relationships as God calls us to do.

7. **Joseph ultimately saw God's hand at work in his suffering and betrayal. How can understanding this perspective help us approach difficult situations in our own lives?**

- Joseph's perspective allowed him to forgive and recognize that his suffering had a divine purpose. By viewing our hardships as part of God's greater plan, we can find peace, knowing that God can use every situation for good. This outlook helps us face trials with faith, trusting that God's purposes will prevail.

8. **How does the concept of the Feast of Atonement deepen our understanding of Joseph's act of forgiveness toward his brothers and their family's restoration?**
    - The Feast of Atonement emphasizes repentance, forgiveness, and restored relationships, aligning with Joseph's forgiveness and reconciliation with his family. Joseph's actions reflect the heart of the feast: a commitment to mercy, healing, and unity. This teaches us that forgiveness isn't just personal but part of God's plan to heal and restore families and communities.

Chapter 13: Reflecting On Joseph's Life And Trials —A Foreshadowing Of The 6Th Seal

1. **How does Joseph's journey of betrayal, suffering, and redemption foreshadow the events of the 6th Seal?**
    - Joseph's trials parallel the cosmic upheaval in the 6th Seal, symbolizing the testing of faith that precedes God's deliverance. His endurance mirrors the steadfastness required of believers as they await God's ultimate redemption during tribulation.

2. **How can Joseph's example of faithfulness inspire us to endure during times of spiritual testing or**

hardship?

- Joseph's unwavering faith, despite betrayals and trials, demonstrates the importance of trusting in God's sovereignty. His example encourages us to remain faithful, knowing that God is refining us and preparing us for a greater purpose.

3. **How does Joseph's reconciliation with his brothers reflect God's desire to reconcile with His people?**
    - Joseph's forgiveness illustrates God's longing for restoration with humanity. Just as Joseph's grace brought his family together, God's forgiveness through Christ invites us back into fellowship with Him, offering redemption and peace.

Chapter 14: Joseph—A Life Of Endurance, Preparation, And Reconciliation

1. **How does Joseph's life exemplify the need for endurance in times of suffering?**
    - Joseph's perseverance through trials—betrayal, slavery, and imprisonment—illustrates a deep trust in God. His endurance shows how faith can sustain us even in bleak circumstances, teaching that God's presence can bring purpose to suffering.

2. **What does Joseph's approach to preparation teach us about stewardship?**
    - Joseph's preparation during years of abundance, storing grain for the famine, reflects a model of foresight and responsibility. This teaches us to be good stewards of both physical and spiritual

resources, preparing for future challenges.

3. **How can reconciliation in Joseph's story inspire reconciliation in our own lives?**
    - Joseph's willingness to forgive his brothers shows how reconciliation involves grace and patience. His example encourages us to let go of past hurts and to restore broken relationships, mirroring God's forgiveness.

Chapter 15: The Role Of Faith Amidst Tribulations

1. **How does Joseph's faith sustain him throughout his trials?**
    - Joseph's unwavering belief that God was with him allowed him to remain resilient. This faith amidst tribulation exemplifies the importance of trusting in God's sovereignty even when circumstances seem unfavorable.

2. **In what ways does Joseph's endurance foreshadow the endurance needed by believers?**
    - Joseph's life is a testament to staying faithful through adversity. This foreshadowing reminds believers that trials refine faith, building endurance in preparation for greater spiritual responsibilities.

Chapter 16: Divine Wisdom In Leadership

1. **What role does divine wisdom play in Joseph's rise to power?**
    - Joseph's ability to interpret Pharaoh's dreams and provide solutions illustrates divine

wisdom. His leadership shows that reliance on God's insight equips us to make decisions that positively impact others.

2. **How can we apply Joseph's reliance on divine wisdom to our daily lives?**
    - By seeking God's guidance in decision-making, as Joseph did, we can make wiser choices. This reliance on divine wisdom encourages believers to look to God for clarity in complex situations.

Chapter 17: Forgiveness As A Path To Reconciliation

1. **Why does Joseph test his brothers before fully reconciling with them?**
    - Joseph's testing is meant to reveal their changed hearts. This process shows that true reconciliation requires both repentance and transformation.
2. **How does Joseph's forgiveness reflect God's forgiveness toward humanity?**
    - Joseph's gracious response to his brothers mirrors God's forgiveness. Just as Joseph welcomed his brothers back, God offers forgiveness and welcomes us into relationship with Him.

Chapter 18: Preparation For Physical And Spiritual Provision

1. **How does Joseph's provision during the famine symbolize spiritual preparation?**

- Joseph's storage of grain represents the foresight to meet future needs. Spiritually, this illustrates the call to nurture faith and prepare our hearts to endure spiritual "famines" or dry periods.

2. **In what ways can believers prepare for spiritual challenges like Joseph prepared for the famine?**
    - Believers can strengthen their faith through prayer, study, and obedience. Like Joseph's strategic planning, spiritual preparation allows us to rely on God during difficult times.

Chapter 19: The Prophetic Nature Of Joseph's Life

1. **How does Joseph's life serve as a prophetic type of Christ's role as Savior?**
    - Joseph's provision for Egypt during famine and his reconciliation with his family parallel Christ's role in offering salvation and restoring humanity to God.
2. **What lessons can we draw from the parallels between Joseph's life and biblical prophecy?**
    - Joseph's life highlights themes of redemption and reconciliation that are fulfilled in Christ. These parallels remind us that God's plan is often revealed progressively, through patterns and types.

Chapter 20: Trusting God's Sovereign Plan

1. **How does Joseph's life demonstrate trust in God's sovereignty?**
    - Despite numerous setbacks, Joseph trusted

in God's ultimate plan. His life illustrates that, though we may not understand our circumstances, God's purposes will unfold.

2. **How can we apply trust in God's sovereignty in our own lives?**
   - By believing that God works for our good, even in trials, we can face difficulties with confidence that they serve a greater purpose.

Chapter 21: Reflecting On Redemption And Restoration

1. **What role does redemption play in Joseph's story?**
   - Joseph's life is a story of redemption—restored family relationships, forgiven past wrongs, and God's grace. This redemption offers hope that broken relationships can be healed.
2. **How does the theme of restoration in Joseph's story relate to God's ultimate plan for humanity?**
   - Joseph's restoration with his family foreshadows the reconciliation God desires with humanity. This theme reflects God's overarching plan to restore creation through Christ.

Chapter 22: Joseph's Legacy As A Model Of Faith

1. **What aspects of Joseph's life form his legacy?**
   - Joseph's faithfulness, wisdom, and forgiveness create a legacy that endures as a model for believers. His life reminds us that true legacy is built on character and faith.
2. **How can believers apply Joseph's legacy of faith to**

their lives today?
- Joseph's legacy encourages us to cultivate faith and integrity, knowing that our actions today impact future generations.

Chapter 23: Lessons In Humility And Obedience

1. **What role does humility play in Joseph's journey?**
   - Despite his high position, Joseph remained humble and acknowledged God's role in his success. His humility serves as a reminder that true greatness is rooted in service to others.
2. **How does obedience shape Joseph's relationship with God?**
   - Joseph's willingness to follow God's guidance, even in hardship, demonstrates the importance of obedience. This obedience laid the foundation for God's blessings in his life.

Chapter 24: Hope In The Face Of Adversity

1. **How does Joseph's story provide hope for those facing adversity?**
   - Joseph's journey from suffering to triumph shows that God is with us in all circumstances. His story provides hope that trials can lead to purpose and blessing.
2. **What can we learn from Joseph's ability to trust in God despite his hardships?**
   - Joseph's trust exemplifies unwavering faith, inspiring us to rely on God even when we cannot see the full picture.

Chapter 25: The Final Reconciliation

1. **How does the final reconciliation between Joseph and his brothers mirror God's reconciliation with humanity?**
    - This reunion illustrates the forgiveness and grace God offers. Joseph's acceptance of his brothers reflects God's love and His desire to reconcile with us.
2. **What does Joseph's story teach us about God's desire for unity within families and communities?**
    - Joseph's reconciliation with his family highlights God's heart for unity and healing. This calls believers to pursue peace and restoration in their own relationships.

SCRIPTURE INDEX

- **Genesis 37:3-4**
  Joseph's favored status and the jealousy of his brothers.
  (Chapter 1: Favored Son, Betrayed Brother)
- **Genesis 37:18-28**
  Joseph is thrown into the pit and sold into slavery.
  (Chapter 2: The Pit and the 6th Seal—Shaken but Not Destroyed)
- **Genesis 39:1-23**
  Joseph's time in Potiphar's house and his unjust imprisonment.
  (Chapter 3: From Prison to Power—The Endurance of the Saints)
- **Genesis 41:1-57**
  Joseph interprets Pharaoh's dreams and rises to power.
  (Chapter 4: The Trumpet Call of Dreams)
- **Genesis 42:1-38**
  Joseph's brothers come to Egypt for food during the famine.
  (Chapter 5: Famine and Judgment—Preparing for What Is to Come)
- **Genesis 45:1-15**
  Joseph reveals his identity and forgives his brothers.
  (Chapter 6: Joseph's Role as a Savior—The Gathering of the People)
- **Genesis 50:20**
  "You intended to harm me, but God intended it for good..."
  (Chapter 7: Managing the Famine—The Wisdom of Joseph)
- **Leviticus 23:23-25**
  The Feast of Trumpets.

(Chapter 4: The Trumpet Call of Dreams)

- **Leviticus 23:26-32**
  The Day of Atonement.
  (Chapter 6: The Feast of Atonement—Forgiveness and Reconciliation)

- **Revelation 6:12-17**
  The opening of the 6th Seal and the cosmic upheaval.
  (Chapter 2: The Pit and the 6th Seal—Shaken but Not Destroyed; Chapter 8: Reflecting on Joseph's Life and Trials—A Foreshadowing of the 6th Seal)

- **Romans 8:28**
  "In all things, God works for the good of those who love Him..."
  (Chapter 3: From Prison to Power—The Endurance of the Saints)

- **Colossians 1:16-17**
  God's sovereignty over all creation.
  (Preface)

- **Proverbs 19:21**
  "Many are the plans in a person's heart, but it is the Lord's purpose that prevails."
  (Preface)

- **John 15:16**
  "You did not choose me, but I chose you..."
  (Preface)

www.ingramcontent.com/pod-product-compliance
Lightning Source LLC
Chambersburg PA
CBHW070547050426
42450CB00011B/2755